ORGANIC FAITH

A Call to Authentic Christianity

ORGANIC
Faith

RON MITCHELL

Cornerstone Press Chicago
Chicago, Illinois

Published by
Cornerstone Press Chicago
939 W. Wilson Ave.
Chicago, IL 60640
cspress@jpusa.chi.il.us

Printed in the United States of America
Cover and interior layout and design by Pat Peterson/wheatsdesign
ISBN 0-940895-40-4

01 00 99 98 5 4 3 2 1

Library of Congress Cataloging-in-Publication Data

Mitchell, Ronald, 1949–
        Organic faith : a call to authentic Christianity / Ronald Mitchell.
        p.   cm.
        Includes bibliographical references.
        ISBN 0–940895–40–4
        1. Christianity.   2. Mitchell, Ronald, 1949–   . 3. Church and the world.   4. Mission of the church.   5. Church and social problems.
        I. Title.
BR124.M57   1997
243—dc21   97–45634
                                                                                        CIP

Three people who had a great influence on me:

My father, Warren E. Mitchell (1922–1995)
Tom Skinner (1942–1994)
Jacques Ellul (1912–1994)

Special thanks to:

My wife, Velma, for her encouragement and help in editing.
So many friends who have contributed greatly to my life.
And above all, to God who inspired this project.

CONTENTS

INTRODUCTION

Jesus Christ touched my life in 1969 while I was a student attending a commuter college in my hometown of New York City. I grew up in a poor neighborhood of Manhattan. My father drove a taxicab and for many years "home" was an apartment in a public housing project. My parents struggled financially in order to escape the gangs, drugs, and violent crime which were becoming more and more a part of our daily surroundings. When I was sixteen years old, my family moved to the outskirts of the Bronx, to an area where people owned the houses they lived in, there were better schools, and it was generally quiet at night. However, this new community was in an early stage of "white flight." Many people living there were fearful of people of other races and cultures moving in; for that reason they competed so as not to be among the last to leave.

The 1960s were a time of social turbulence in the United States. The civil rights movement was giving way to talk of black power. There was an emerging counterculture and there were murmurings of revolution in the air. Cities across the

United States were experiencing riots. The Vietnam War was raging. None of these things were merely distant issues flashed on the evening news. It was all very close to home. I grew up with a good friend named Jack. We went to the same high school and were members of the same Boy Scout troop. As teenagers we socialized, often playing chess together at his apartment on Saturday mornings. The news that he had been shot in the head and killed in the jungles of Vietnam hit me very hard. Also, around this time, I developed a romantic relationship with a teenage girl in our church youth fellowship. She was white. When her family became aware of the relationship, their reaction included verbal threats to harm me physically.

Accept Jesus Christ in my life? My girlfriend's father was one of the leaders in the church. He even claimed to have given his life to Christ at an evangelistic rally years before. When my black radical friends voiced that Christianity was the white man's religion, it was not easy to dismiss what they were saying. It was very apparent to me that the world around me was not what it should be. Among other things, I became convinced that negative conditions such as those found in the inner city could be changed. So I committed myself to working for social change. At first this commitment was based on romantic idealism. It didn't take long for me to realize that "chasing windmills" like Don Quixote would have little effect on society's deeply entrenched evils. Also, how could one change the world when one's own life needed changing? God worked in my life through the witness of a number of Christians and the searching of the Scriptures. God showed me that, ultimately, it was only through Jesus Christ that both my life and society could be changed.

Integration of social justice and evangelism was never just some kind of academic exercise in my life as a Christian. At the point of committing my life to Christ, I knew that true Christianity combined both the messages of Billy Graham and Martin Luther King Jr. Even in the midst of difficulty in my interracial relationship, there was a glimpse of Jesus Christ standing over and against what I was seeing in the behavior of Christians. When my girlfriend's father was challenged to apply his Christianity to our dating situation, his response was that one could not take Christianity seriously in this case. That told me something about what it would be like if one really did take Christianity seriously.

I soon met others in InterVarsity Christian Fellowship (IVCF)[1] who shared this concern for the whole gospel—one that combined evangelism with social concern. While a college student, I struggled with the issue of why so many white Christians, including those who claimed to be "born-again," seemed just as prejudiced as those not claiming to be Christians. How was I to explain Bob Jones University, a Christian college where there was a policy to keep black people out? One learned that it was so much easier to integrate lunch counters than it was to integrate churches. How did this come about? As a sociology major, I geared my research opportunities towards examining this question. Through reading about the response of churches to slavery and segregation in the

United States, it became clear to me that most white churches did nothing to fight racism; on the contrary, they even helped to foster it.

InterVarsity played a major part in my nurture and personal growth as a Christian. During the time I was active in Metro New York IVCF, we were challenged to show the college world that Christianity related not only to what professors taught in the classrooms, but also to the issues of racism, inner-city poverty, and the Vietnam War. We had to respond to pronouncements by our peers that Christianity was merely a tool of oppression. In the late 1960s and early 1970s IVCF students in New York City prayed and struggled together with these questions. We also stirred up the larger IVCF movement.

I became chapter president of the Lehman College Christian fellowship group, which was affiliated with IVCF, and was later elected chairperson of the New York City student area committee. The area committee took seriously that IVCF was a student-led movement. We planned and organized conferences and began to challenge the larger InterVarsity movement to look at the social implications of the gospel.

At this time, IVCF students were expected to read Francis Schaeffer, a leading Christian theologian, along with their Bible. New York InterVarsity students read both and went further to say that Christian apologetics also had to explain Christian participation in slavery, segregation, and other kinds of social injustice. In the various workshops we organized, many of these issues were addressed. A few of us even raised issues with the Reverend Billy Graham as he organized a crusade at New York's Shea Stadium in 1970. In a preparatory meeting with him and Christian youth representatives, a number of us confronted him about his close identification with then-president Richard Nixon. There was a general perception that he was giving full endorsement to Nixon's policies on the Vietnam War and on domestic issues. At the meeting, we also pressed Billy Graham to relate his crusade messages to issues affecting people living in the inner cities.

Furthermore, New York City students made their mark at the Urbana 1970 Student Missionary Convention.[2] A black caucus was organized which met after the evening plenary sessions. As the person leading the first meeting, a feeling of total inadequacy overtook me at the onset. Before those gathered could focus on any issues, it was suggested that the white people in the room be asked to leave. A heated debate broke out but was soon interrupted with the beginning of a workshop on black Americans in mission. Moderated by Bill Pannell, that workshop was to have an impact on me years later when called to go overseas. But at that moment in time, the difficult issue of whether or not to exclude whites from the caucus pressed on me.

God was speaking in a profound way in those minutes as staff worker Paul Gibson and others prayed with me. It was not enough to be involved in social change because of a Christian commitment. Without strength and direction from Christ, that social concern was devoid of real power. The lesson was being learned that just because one was sensitive to certain issues didn't mean that one would always have the right approach to resolving them. Tom Skinner, an African-American evangelist, was soon called in to the black caucus. He took leadership of the sessions from that point. It was eventually decided to ask those who were not of African descent to be excused. However, they were invited to participate jointly in the last session.

Christians who wake up to social concern many times fall into a trap. We become overly impressed by non-Christians who are committed to eradicating injustices. We begin to see them as models. But I was learning through the challenges of this caucus that Christian social action is something different from a carbon copy of the activity of others. Jesus Christ doesn't give us a blank check to do anything we want to just because we are addressing a wrong in society.

The message that the social concern of Christians should be different from that of others was being impressed upon me in other ways while active in IVCF. At my fellowship meeting at Lehman College, Tom Howard (known then as the author of *Christ the Tiger*) was invited to conduct a workshop. During the session I described my part-time job as a tenant organizer, struggling to uplift the conditions of low-class tenement buildings in the South Bronx. Those who owned the buildings didn't live in them. These landlords basically collected rent for run-down buildings which they neglected to repair. Even in the middle of winter, families in these buildings would go without heat and hot water for extended periods of time. I revealed in the meeting that I felt God's call to this work. I also mentioned that I was teamed up with another college student who was Jewish, who did not act out of any religious convictions.

Although I noted that I had found some opportunities to share my faith with my coworker, Tom Howard continued to press the question of what difference being a Christian made in my activism.

I have had opportunities to serve in mission both in the inner city of New York and overseas as a missionary. In my current work, I direct a church-affiliated homeless shelter in White Plains, New York. Through the years, I have continued to struggle with the question of the difference it makes to be a Christian involved in social concern. It seems that while many Christians get involved in addressing social issues because they see God calling them to this concern, too often they leave Jesus Christ behind as they engage in practical action. As a result, their practical action mirrors that of activists who are not motivated by Christian faith.

God is still working on me. For some time now I have felt that God wants me to share the things I have learned on my pilgrimage with those who are struggling in the same way. The chapters which follow are to be considered more like the spokes of a wheel rather than a linear progression. The center hub is the theme that Christians are called by Christ to make a real difference in the world. My prayer is that what is said will help readers to live out God's heavenly kingdom more faithfully here on earth.

1

A SPLIT-LEVEL GOSPEL

The dichotomy between evangelism and real-life concern for others is one of the most serious problems impeding Christianity as it enters the new millennium. Some churches are concerned about social evils and the plight of suffering people, but have little or no interest in personal evangelism. On the other hand, many churches are committed to evangelism without concern for the poor or those suffering under oppression. This "split-level" gospel, paraded before the world, works paradoxically against both evangelism and social concern at the same time. Because today's world confronts us with issues of poverty, political repression, war, ethnic conflicts, and environmental destruction—painful realities for so many people—evangelism is hindered when Christians show little or no concern for these realities. For many non-Christians it is not the "scandal of the cross" that causes them to reject

Christianity. Rather, what turns them off is the scandalous indifference of Christians.

How have Christians left themselves open to this kind of criticism? How did the split occur between evangelism and social concern? The weak social witness of Western-world Christianity can be traced to two dangerous trends. One is the tendency to misuse Christian teachings to accommodate and support the status quo. The other is the tendency to separate Christian faith from various social issues. Both of these produce the same effects: social evil and injustice in the world are left unchallenged and our Christian witness is weakened. Examples of how these scandals work are numerous.

For instance, many Jewish people are open to experimentation with other religions, but will not consider the claims of Christianity. In light of the complicity of the German church in the Holocaust, it is easy to see how the credibility of the gospel was damaged. In the United States, the living legacy of racism must be addressed for any Christian outreach to African-Americans to be successful. In fact, our inability to address racism enables Louis Farrakhan and his Nation of Islam movement to make advances by pointing out how Christianity has been used to keep black people down.

In recent history, Bishop Desmond Tutu exemplified a Christian who refused to accommodate or segregate his beliefs. Bishop Tutu was a leading voice of opposition to South Africa's apartheid system in the 1980s. As he spoke out against this system of forced racial segregation and inequality, he found people telling him: "Don't mix religion with politics!" He found it strange that this criticism was only raised when religious people were opposing some unjust policy. On the other hand, he observed that "if that same policy is described by religious leaders as being in accordance with Christianity, then there is no question [raised] . . . of mixing religion with politics."[1] Although Tutu is a shining example, the sad fact is that his integrity is exception to the rule. There are many instances in which Christians, unlike Tutu, freely compromise their beliefs when faced with social evil and injustice.

Modifying Beliefs To Maintain Slavery

This tendency to accommodate and segregate Christian beliefs is illustrated in the experience of African-Americans as they encountered racism in the United States. As we go back and look at the historical record, especially the relationship of white Protestantism with black people in America, the general pattern is one of discrepancy between genuine Christian creed and real-life deeds. The historian David Reimers gives this assessment of the time up through the 1960s: " 'Whites Only' was never carved over the door of any white Protestant church in America; it was understood." The white Protestant church generally gave support to both slavery and segregation.[2] And although there have been significant changes since the Civil Rights era, studies still show little difference between the racial attitudes of the average churchgoer and that of the general population.

During the 1660s, when slavery was beginning to emerge in the American English colonies, a controversy erupted in the churches regarding its practice. There was an unwritten English law that a Christian could not be enslaved. Because of this understanding, slave owners initially discouraged any effort to convert slaves to Christianity as it could result in their release from slavery.[3] In order to maintain slavery, laws were created to allow a slave to become a Christian and still remain a slave. In 1729, the English Court upheld these laws by ruling that "baptism could not alter the temporal condition of a slave within the British Kingdom."[4] This ruling especially affected what was taking place in the American colonies.

In the early days of slavery, evangelism took second place to the work of promoting and maintaining slavery. Only after it was accepted that slaves who became Christians would remain slaves were there major efforts to evangelize them. The churches then further accommodated this evil by giving their approval to slavery. When slaves were given religious instruction, they heard that slavery had divine sanction. Disobedience was as much an offense against God as against the slave master. Bible verses were used to reinforce the belief that servants should obey their masters or else punishments would await the disobedient slave in the afterlife. The slaves were also promised that eternal salvation would be their reward for faithful service.[5] Slaves were prohibited from learning how to read the Bible for themselves.[6]

People came forward with various religious justifications for slavery, especially in the years following the American Revolutionary War. These justifications came in response to the challenge of abolitionists in the northern states. Many abolitionists had based their opposition to slavery on Christian faith and teaching. In response, one of the justifications given to uphold slavery was that blacks were soulless, subhuman beings. Some people even rationalized that it was a Christian's duty not to impede the fulfillment of Noah's curse on his son Ham and this meant enslaving and oppressing black people.[7] These teachings sanctioned almost any ill treatment of blacks by the larger society.

Although slavery ended with the American Civil War, the justifications for racial oppression continued on. Years after the Civil War, at the turn of the century, large numbers of Charles Carroll's *The Negro a Beast* were published and circulated by the American Book and Bible House. In this publication, Carroll used Scripture to defend the view that blacks were soulless beasts and that a Christian's only duty to them was to repress and degrade them.[8] Slavery had ended. Yet, the distorted Christian teachings which encouraged racial prejudice remained in place.

Slavery was outlawed in the northern states before the Civil War, but most white churches there adopted the practice of segregation. Blacks sat confined in certain sections of the church and were separated from whites for the administration of communion. Churches in the South also adopted the practice of segregation after the war. African-Americans were banned from membership in many churches. There were never any laws which required segregation in churches. However, the poor example set by these churches helped pave the way for legalized segregation in the southern states.[9]

Even in the 1960s, many stories were told of white missionaries returning home from Africa with African converts who were refused admission into the missionaries' own supporting churches. While I served as a missionary in Sierra Leone, a bishop of a national church shared with me his experience as a student coming to the United States. Although the experience had taken place years before, a lasting impression had been made on him. A white missionary accompanying him on his ship had been very friendly and supportive as they prepared for their arrival in the United States. But when the ship landed in Norfolk, Virginia, the missionary disappeared without warning or explanation. This young student was left alone not knowing how to get around. He further discovered through this rude experience the reality of segregation as he tried to flag down white taxi drivers who all passed him by.

Many independent black churches and denominations developed in the northern states in protest to the segregationist practices of white Protestant churches. These African-American churches fought against slavery and inequality. These churches experienced phenomenal growth as former slaves joined in great numbers following the Civil War.[10] The black church generally distinguished two types of Christianity: one which was used to justify slavery and racial prejudice and another which was faithful to the gospel. Frederick Douglas, an escaped slave who became an abolitionist and an ordained preacher in the African Methodist Episcopal Zion (AMEZ) Church, made such a distinction in his speeches. He called the Christianity of America "a religion for oppressors, tyrants, man stealers and thugs," which was unlike the "pure and impartial Christianity of Christ."[11]

The justifications given by churches to the immoral and inhuman institution of slavery came after the fact. Economic, political, and social forces generated and fueled the establishment of slavery; the support of churches came about in order to accommodate to it.[12] In order to make arguments to rationalize slavery, the very theology of the church was modified. The maintenance of slavery became a matter of church doctrine for the churchgoer; even after slavery had ended with the Civil War, the religious justifications stayed on to foster racism.

Segregating Beliefs

An accommodation to the trends of the larger society is a characteristic of many churches. Such churches serve to maintain uncritically the institutions and the interests of the larger society.[13] While accommodation to social evil can come about by modifying beliefs, it can also come about by segregating beliefs. This pattern of conformity has been researched and documented in numerous sociological studies.

A classic study was done on the clergy's actions during the Little Rock crisis of the 1950s.[14] Here national attention and United States federal troops were brought to the city of Little Rock, Arkansas, during the early days of the civil rights struggle. The local authorities refused to comply with court-ordered school desegregation. In the study of the local white clergy's response, it was found that the clergy generally disassociated their religious and moral values from the issue of segregation. In this case, they safely separated belief from action rather than giving a justification for racial segregation.

A parallel is found in the response of many German churches to Hitler. Historians note that Hitler could not have gone as far as he did without the tacit support of the German church. Some German Christians actually tried to accommodate their beliefs with the Nazi program. Most others went along by simply segregating their personal beliefs from what was taking place around them. "Hitler insisted that the church restrict itself to matters of personal salvation and not become involved in concerns of the state. To the extent that the churches were willing to make that bargain, they were protected by the Third Reich. They were left alone, free to worship however and whenever they pleased, as long as they agreed to the one constraint."[15] Hitler once told a German pastor, "You take care of people's souls, I will take care of their bodies."

Getting to the Roots

There has always been a minority within Western churches acting against racism and other social evils on the basis of their Christian commitment. Studies by social psychologists show that people approach their religious beliefs in different ways. These studies, built on Gordon Allport's pivotal research, revealed that "those who were considered the most devout, more personally absorbed in their religion, were far less prejudiced than . . . [those with] the institutional type of attachment, external and political in nature."[16]

In *Varieties of Religious Experiences,* William James asserts cynically that "piety is the mask, the inner force is tribal instinct."[17] The pull of selfish motivation, in addition and interlocked with societal pressures, propels many Christians to become accomplices to social evil and injustice. Like everyone else, we as Christians have a tendency to conform to our society and social groups. (This tendency to conform also motivates Christians to support the positive aspects of our societies. Church people, for example, are usually law-abiding.) But real Christianity is much more than mere social conformity.

What makes up the pressures of society to which Christians are tempted to succumb? What are the resources of real Christianity which can help us to withstand these pressures? Social scientists point out three basic forces operating in society that have a compelling control over people's behavior. These are economic, political, and social and, while the effect of each can vary from one society to another, they are very dominating. Look carefully and we can see that they are the essence of Satan's temptation of Christ in the wilderness (see Luke 4:1–13). Satan's strategy with us, as with Christ, is not only to make us fear the inexorable power of these three forces, but also to tempt us to turn them into idols—things which we pursue as ends in themselves.

Economics breaks down to the simple question of "what will we eat and wear and where will we find shelter?" This force involves our physical needs. It involves things we are anxious about not having. While fearful of doing without, we are also tempted into materialism. For example, we might be satisfied by our company's discriminatory practices if we are part of a privileged racial, ethnic, or gender group working in that business company. The material comforts we receive benefit us. At the same time, we do not want put at risk a job that feeds our family by going against our company's unjust practices. We need food, clothing, and shelter. Yet, Jesus rejects Satan's use of this force to tempt him in the wilderness. He puts God's will first; "the Scriptures say: 'No one can live only on food'" (Luke 4:4b CEV). The economic temptation is to simply keep us from seeking first God's kingdom.

Next, Satan appeals to Christ with an offer of the world's kingdoms. However, what Satan offers is, in the words of Communist Chinese leader Mao, the power that "comes out of the barrel of a gun." When the political state has the power to coerce with lethal force, people tend to go along and mute their opposition. Since those who disobey face punishment and possibly death, political power conveys a kind of reverence similar to worship. The early Christians faced the pressure of Caesar worship. They were persecuted and killed when they didn't comply. The Romans would have allowed them to practice their own religion as long as they participated in Caesar worship. In fact, some did compromise in this way. But there is a difference between a healthy respect for governmental authority (Romans 13) and worship of authority (Revelation 13). It is said that whatever it is we are uncritical towards, be it government or anything else, becomes our god.[18] History shows too many cases of Christians going along with others to turn a political entity—be it a person, a system, or a nationalist group—into a god. Jesus rejects the pull of such power as he answers Satan with the scripture, "Worship the Lord your God and serve only him!" (Luke 4:8b CEV).

Finally, Satan utilizes social status, our desires to be accepted by others and our worries about what people think about us. Just like food, human beings have a basic psychological need to be accepted, not just by some large crowd, but also by family, friends, and smaller in-groups. Racism developed among whites in the United States not only for economic reasons; poor whites did not own slaves, yet they cultivated racist attitudes because there was societal "acceptance" for doing so. If a particular social group is the only prop for one's psychological sense of worth and value, then that person is as dependent on that group as an addict is dependent on drugs. It is difficult to resist conformity when it fills such a basic psychological need.

Satan offered Christ the appeal of an elevated social prestige. He tempted Christ to jump off the highest point of the temple so as to prove he was the Son of God (Luke 4:9–12). That act would have been the equivalent of a present day media mega-event, providing a tremendous lift in public approval ratings. Jesus rejects this temptation to seek status in and of itself. The good news is that Christ offers a new status as children of God to those who accept Him (John 1:12). When society makes someone its orphan, God the Father, Son, and Holy Spirit is there to adopt that person. Then, as a child of God, that person is provided a supportive family through the fellowship of believers.

The Bible and Social Injustice

In spite of the modification and segregation of Christian beliefs to accommodate social injustice, the Bible stands unequivocally against both social and personal sin. God opposes those who oppress the poor, the stranger, the weak, and the destitute. We read in Isaiah 41:17, "The poor and needy search for water, but there is none; their tongues are parched with thirst. But I the Lord will answer them; I, the God of Israel, will not forsake them" (NIV).

God takes offense at oppressive societies denying justice to the poor. He opposes courts of law favoring the rich and powerful over the poor and weak. Judgment awaits those who show no compassion towards the poor. In Isaiah 3:14-15 we read, "The Lord enters into judgment against the elders and leaders of his people: 'It is you who have ruined my vineyard; the plunder from the poor is in your houses. What do you mean by crushing my people and grinding the faces of the poor?' declares the Lord, the LORD Almighty" (NIV). In the book of James, we read about judgment for those who "have hoarded wealth in the last days." James tells them: "Look! The wages you failed to pay the workmen who mowed your fields are crying out against you. The cries of the harvesters have reached the ears of the Lord Almighty" (James 5:4 NIV).

In the Gospel of Luke, Jesus begins his ministry proclaiming, "The Lord's Spirit has come to me, because he has chosen me to tell the good news to the poor. The Lord has sent me to announce freedom for prisoners, to give sight to the blind, to free everyone who suffers, and to say 'This is the year the Lord has chosen.' " (Luke 4:18–19 CEV). A powerful message. Jesus is good news for the poor and the oppressed. But when the world looks at Western Christianity, it receives a diluted message.

Rediscovering Wholistic Christianity

Not all Christians in Western history have watered down the gospel by accommodating and segregating beliefs. Up until the twentieth century, those in the forefront of evangelistic mission and spiritual revival were also actively working to alleviate the suffering of the poor and oppressed. The slavery abolitionist movement was led by many people who today would be described as Evangelicals.[19] The Methodist revival of John Wesley was permeated with social concern. The sociologist David Moberg has described the shedding of social concern by Evangelicals during the early part of this century as "the great reversal."[20]

Many Christians are recovering the tradition of integrating social concern and evangelism.[21] As a missionary in West Africa, I was inspired by the national church with which I was working. They had a passion for evangelistic outreach to Muslims and other nonbelievers *and* were engaged in developing schools, literacy programs, health centers, vocational training programs, and other community development projects serving the poor. A strong commitment to wholistic ministry is found among Christians in developing countries. These ideas and practices are being reintroduced into the mainstream of evangelical churches in the West in ways that reach beyond the closed systems of the past eight decades.

Blank Check Theology

In the preceding sections I have focused on the errors of modifying beliefs in order to support the status quo. However, there are errors on the other side of the political divide as well. The teaching of the Bible is clearly against the injustice of systems perpetuating poverty and oppression, but some take these teachings to be a "blank check" as they address social and cultural concerns. This has been a tendency for much of liberation theology. People are encouraged to attach themselves uncritically to secular movements involved in social activism.

Latin American theologians have been at the forefront of developing a "theology of liberation" over the past few decades. African-American theologians who have written on "black theology" and others, including feminist theologians, are also sometimes identified as liberation theologians. Although the proponents of liberation theology vary greatly in their views, all share the common concern of addressing issues of oppression and social injustice.

James Cone has been in the forefront of black theology in the United States. He sees the weakness of churches in the United States arising from the way they have accommodated to the dominant society. By doing this, Cone contends, the churches has supported the interests of the oppressors rather than the oppressed.[22] However, Cone offers little guidance as to how the Christian's response to racism should be different from that of a secular response. He does not distinguish clearly between God's identification with the oppressed and God's conformity with the means the oppressed may use to liberate themselves. According to Cone, it seems that God approves of all forms of sociopolitical liberation, including those that may employ authoritarian or even violent remedies.

Liberation theologians in Latin America are focused on the institutional exploitation and oppression facing so many people in their societies. Yet some of these theologians go further to embrace Marxism as both an analysis of and a solution to such problems.[23] While liberation theologians rightly call our attention to social sins, many end up embracing non-Christian courses of action. They seemingly rule out the possibility of Christians adopting their own unique course of action. Instead, we are pulled to conform to a particular secular movement and then use the Bible to justify it.[24]

The Challenge Before Us

While Christians can work within many secular movements, the challenge is to discover a uniquely Christian social concern. Such a concern must center itself on Jesus Christ. He is the reason for our motivation. He is the One who gives us power to act. And it is Christ who directs our actions in the world. We should not be Christians on the one hand and then uncritically turn to secular philosophies and social movements in order to offer hope to the world.[25]

Communism had claimed to liberate the poor and oppressed. People clung to it religiously because they believed it was going to end economic injustice. It would usher in a new society in which the poor would no longer be poor and exploitation would be a thing of the past. It had a strong moral appeal. Communism was hailed, not just as a way to organize the economic system more fairly, but as an all-embracing worldview and philosophy of life. People were willing to kill for it. People were willing to sacrifice their lives to bring about this new order.

But it didn't work. The myth that Communism is the answer to the world's problems exploded in front of the whole world. Karl Marx had described religion as the "opiate of the people" with Christianity as one of Marx's major targets. The irony is that the twentieth century will be remembered in part as the one in which Communism showed itself to be an opiate with destructive and dehumanizing effects on the very people it was said to help.

As Communism fell around the world during the early 1990s, the vacuum it created needed to be filled. But little has been offered as a vision for a new society. The liberated peoples of the former Soviet Union and Eastern Europe are now free from a system that proved to be unworkable. While the peoples of Eastern Europe look for answers, most do not see Christianity as a vision for changing the social system.[26] Instead, ethnic nationalism has emerged as a powerful force. Capitalism, too, is being offered as some kind of miracle cure for the ills of these societies. Rather than offering a new vision, many Christians are again falling into line with the world as they provide both implicit and active support for ethnic nationalisms and capitalism.

American Christians are pleased that they can now carry out missionary work in these former Communist nations. There is a fear, though, that the power of their message will be diminished by accommodations made to support "Americanism." And many at the forefront of this new wave of evangelism are going to these countries with a message devoid of challenges to social injustice. People are hearing only that Christianity is a passport out of hell into heaven; the struggles and realities of everyday life are not being addressed.

The gospel of Jesus Christ needs to be proclaimed with more than just a focus on the hereafter. Real Christianity is not an opiate for people oppressed by social evil. The gospel is revolutionary because it speaks to both the social and personal issues confronting people around the world. The gospel has implications for both here and now and for the hereafter. It speaks to spiritual, emotional, physical, and social concerns, as biblical Christianity is unequivocally wholistic.

Christianity is about a real revolution getting to the heart of the world's problems. Radical movements in the world tend to just rearrange the forces over people's lives instead of challenging them. The money, power, and social prestige which "make the world go 'round" are not questioned by these movements. To be set free in Christ is to be set free to make a real difference in the world.

In the early days of Christianity, people complained that Christians "turned the world upside down" (Acts 17:6 PHILLIPS). The way they lived challenged the society. Christians were not only different because of what they believed, but because what they believed changed the way they lived. Real Christianity is about a radically new society of those living the values of the kingdom of God. In this new society, with Jesus in control, the practice of love, peace, and righteousness sharply contrasts with the worldly practices of the surrounding society. The Bible has bad news for the systems of the world. They are flawed. They are fading away. The good news is that this new society—the kingdom of God—will continue on forever. Unfortunately, many Christians continue to accommodate and uphold the passing systems of the world and so dilute the message of the gospel. In order to regain a uniquely Christian social concern, we must begin to sort out the values of the world from the values of God's kingdom. The first step in doing this requires a clear understanding of the nature of the world in which we live.

2

A WORLD OF
GOOD AND EVIL?

A s I walked along the hot, busy street in the West African
city, a man singled me out, probably recognizing me as a
foreigner. He wanted money, but it was no ordinary illusionary
trick he was performing. The man's face changed shape,
becoming abnormally extended like a cartoon character's. In a
split second it returned to normal. I had heard stories of
witchcraft in Africa, but up until then I had not experienced
anything like this. I felt something very heavy in the atmosphere surrounding him; there was a scent of spiritual evil in the
air. It was as though dark clouds were gathering before a
lightning storm, yet it was broad daylight. The local stories
about him were that he used *juju*, a form of witchcraft, to bend
his face and body into shapes that were otherwise humanly
impossible.

Many times we as Christians are drawn into limiting the way we identify evil. We look for something which stands out from the ordinary, such as a manifestation of black magic. Yet what about those things we have become accustomed to, the many things we take for granted every day? It is much more difficult to see evil operating within our social surroundings. It is especially difficult when our cultural environment sends out both scents of evil and good blended together. To understand our world's predicament and to begin sorting out evil and good, we need to go back to humanity's fall from grace.

In the first chapter of Genesis we are told that human beings were created in God's own image and likeness. Humanity was originally created to reflect God's character both in our individual and communal lives. We mirrored God's pure goodness. But something happened. Something went very wrong.

God had created Homo sapiens to be special. We were given a unique place in creation. Unlike programmed robots or animals living by instinct, humans were given liberty of choice. But the Bible tells us that Adam and Eve chose to disobey God; they ate from the tree of the knowledge of good and evil. Adam and Eve rejected the tree of life which was placed in the center of the Garden. They went against God's will and listened to the tempter. The tree of life represented dependence on God and relationship with God. If they had obeyed God, human life on earth would have been reflective of life in heaven.

A Mixed Bag

The word *knowledge,* used in describing the tree, can be a little confusing. It is assumed to mean *head knowledge.* We tend towards this interpretation due to our Western-mind thinking. A better way of translating this Hebrew word *knowledge* is with the word *experience.*[1] What comes forth from the tree they selected is "the experience of good and evil." With sin now infecting humanity, our world is a mixed bag of good and evil. It is significant that the tree Adam and Eve chose was not one of pure evil. It was good and evil mixed together, coming in a package that could not be sorted out. Isn't this the very history and experience of the world? Both beauty and ugliness exist. In *A Tale of Two Cities* we read, "It was the best of times, it was the worst of times." Try as we may as humans to change it, it seems that our world is stuck with this reality of good and evil intertwined together.

Humans have a basic aversion to recognizing that they are bound to a habitat where good is mixed with evil. We are always being compelled to identify the evil and develop a program to get rid of it, supposedly once and for all. Yet we can't completely shake it off. Not in our personal lives. Not in our communities or in our nations.

The world and our individual lives become like a Shakespearean tragedy with all the different acts going on at the same time: The hope and promise of a newborn baby side by side with a loved one's premature death. Or, "We're in love and getting married; we're really excited." And later, "Things aren't working out; we're separated and my spouse is filing for divorce." Excited about some new political leader going to make a positive change; years later elated about a replacement.

We seek out ways to cope with a world that isn't what it should be. We can be lured into traps *because* things are not completely evil and bad. Like Adam and Eve, we have also tasted something "good" in this fruit. Consequently, we are trapped into thinking that we, on our own, can find the formula to remove the evil part. Some are drawn into various philosophies and movements which promise to eradicate evil. Others feel they can escape evil by simply moving away.

Islands of Refuge

I watched a story on the evening news once about a woman who had left Eastern Europe some years earlier. Tired of the stifling repression of her communistic society and its lack of political liberty, she fled to the United States in hopes of finding a place of freedom and opportunity. Through much hard work she became a medical doctor. But she became involved in her own fatal attraction. Her life was cut short by a former boyfriend who brutally murdered her. She ran from one evil only to find herself the victim of a different kind of evil.

Many of us yearn for a place far from the evils of the world. We want to be free from the evil which comes intertwined with goodness. Years ago people told a story of a certain man who wanted to leave behind modern civilization. This man saw the tensions in the world building up just before World War II. He wanted to get away from it all before things erupted into full-scale war. He sought out an isolated island far from everything.

He settled on a beautiful island in the South Pacific, yet he did not escape. The island became the scene of a bloody and vicious battle during World War II.

Although very few people actually go off to such physical islands, many search out other kinds of islands free of the world's evil. It may be through a philosophy, or a movement. A place where it appears to be possible to finally shake off the evil in the world; somewhere this unbearable tension can be resolved. People want something more out of life—they want a place where good and evil are not inseparably joined. It is as though buried in each person's subconscious is a glimmer of the Garden of Eden, the place we dream of returning to.

Common Myths

Many people get caught up in movements because they promise to set things right. All the different "isms" of the world carry such assurances. When these "isms" finally do come to power, most people begin to realize that they still have not arrived in Eden. Nevertheless, the movement's leaders may still want to hold on to power. Instead of facing up to the fact that their movement hasn't delivered on its promises, these leaders resort to propaganda and the repression of those who point out the movement's failings.

Democratic societies may check the abuses of power and totalitarian ideologies, but they have not returned us to Eden. Injustice, corruption, racism and ethnic hatred, immorality, and crime are problems crying out to be resolved. Some people feel that if society built enough prisons or created enough laws it could rid itself of evil. Others feel that the answer is in government social programs. Neither new laws and prisons nor increased social programs by themselves can solve the problems of our society. It is hard for us to accept that our human attempts to set right the world ultimately fall short. Rather than this, many people get caught up believing in various "myths."[2] Some of these myths may be extreme—as in the promises of Communism or fascism—but many of us are drawn into other myths which we accept as reasonable.

We tend to gravitate towards these reasonable myths in our approaches to our social problems. Many who work with homeless people lock themselves into narrow approaches to the problem. When calling attention to the plight of homeless people, many advocates promote the idea that the only problem is the shortage of affordable housing—minimizing or even dismissing the roles played by alcoholism, drug abuse, and mental illness in contributing to homelessness. As a result, when the government and other organizations provide funding, these particular problems do not get much attention.

Another myth is fostered by stressing that homelessness is solely an issue of personal responsibility. Bringing up the neglected issues, these advocates often don't face the problem of affordable housing. Both sides settle into separate approaches, with neither one fully addressing all the problems faced by homeless people. This is how we buy into "solutions" which we try to hold onto even after they have proven not to work.

For society as a whole, science and technology form the basis of one grand unexamined assumption, a belief that given time, the world of the future will resolve the problems that face humanity. Jacques Ellul considers the "power-image" of progress as "one of the major mythical aspects of our time." We have an unquestioned faith that "science cannot but lead us from progress to progress."[3] While we attach a stigma to Communists or fascists pursuing their visions of a new world order, society is very accepting of scientific and technological myths.

Many of us are also captivated by a belief in the effectiveness of military power to remove evil from the world. Going to war takes on the quality of a spiritual crusade which will "finally" crush evil. When the price of sacrifice has been paid and the guns are silent, we are told that now we can have peace. We celebrate our troops coming home; there is a hope in the air for world peace. This was the feeling that people had at the end of the "Great War," World War I. It was repeated after World War II, and was expressed again with the fall of the Berlin Wall and what former president Ronald Reagan called the "evil empire." It seems that we are always hearing about that "war to end all wars." Over and over it is said, "People will now learn their lesson and not do those things that bring on wars." Although it doesn't happen, war and violence continue to be touted as ways to bring about justice and make peace in the world.

History plays out again and again the dashed hopes that we will somehow rid ourselves of the consequences of humanity's fall from grace. The wise historian will tell you that history teaches us that people do not learn from history. We want to find the road back to the Garden of Eden, but our routes seem like a never-ending maze. Each time we see glimpses of peace in the world, some new problem pops up. Every time we get ready to sit down and relax, there is a new crisis. Turning our backs on God and choosing our own way, we became stuck with this "knowledge of good and evil."

Beyond Simplistic Labels

During my early years in college, before committing my life to Christ, I was intrigued by this philosophical question: is humanity basically evil or basically good? Reading the novels of Joseph Conrad fueled my thinking; Conrad brings out the point that much of what is taken for granted as Western "civilization" is in reality a cloak hiding venal and murderous "uncivilized" drives. Film director Francis Ford Coppola applied Conrad's *Heart of Darkness* to his Vietnam War film, *Apocalypse Now*. The point is made that individuals or societies cannot be simplistically labeled as either good or evil. There is usually some good to be found in many of the things we label as "bad" and some bad to be found in so much of what we label as "good."

It is rare to hear Christian preachers speaking about the world in terms of good and bad mixed together. We tend to communicate only the bad side in order to be effective. Yet this reinforces our tendency towards simplistic "all good" and "all bad" judgments. Whereas there are many things deserving of such good and bad labeling, most of what takes place in the world cannot be easily classified in this way. Christians often fall into a trap because of this kind of thinking. This has also been the tendency of many of us when dealing with social issues.

Much of the debate over evangelism versus social action reflects this.[4] According to this way of thinking, if you find fault with something, it justifies throwing out the whole. If you are for social concern, then you can ignore what people concerned about evangelism are saying. You know they are wrong in their social views and so that justifies throwing out anything else they might have to say. If you are for evangelism, ignore whatever those in favor of social concern are saying because they are not interested in the spiritual welfare of others.

People are drawn to categorize and stereotype presumably because this helps them to cope with a complicated world. Propaganda and media manipulation are made possible because of this need to simplify. It works because there is the drive to resolve the "mixed bag" reality of the world. Latch onto something we have found as "good" and play down its "bad" aspects. We feel that recognizing and giving attention to its "bad" elements will discredit the "good" parts we are trying to advance. Conversely, we want to minimize any "good" that may be operating within those persons or groups to which we are opposed.

For many, the United States of America is either basically good or basically evil. Some people see America only as a successful beacon of hope in the world, promoting freedom and democracy. For others, it is a place of economic exploitation with racism and militarism glossed over by an attitude of cultural and technological superiority. This calls to mind the argument of whether the glass is half empty or half full. Isn't it really both? And this is generally what the world faces in its experience of good and evil. There is *real* good and *real* evil taking place at the same time. As Ronald Sider points out, "human sin has permeated our social structures and institutions to such a degree that they are always a tragic mixture of good and evil."[5]

In the fall of 1991, Americans were glued to their television sets as the United States Senate engaged in hearings to consider the confirmation of Clarence Thomas as a Supreme Court justice. Anita Hill, a respected law professor, came forward with assertions that she had been sexually harassed by Clarence Thomas while working for him years before. The choice was taken for granted—one had to be right, the other certainly wrong. The issues of politics, sexual harassment, due process, race, and other concerns all seemed to collide at once. The opinions that came forward reflected the pull to categorize and simplify. As a result there were strong attempts to discredit the excellent character witnesses of both Anita Hill and Clarence Thomas.[6] Since that time there have been other cases given media attention in which people are drawn into embracing one side and rejecting the other. It is not always just a case of convenient "fencing" when someone cannot take sides.[7]

When we categorize one side as wrong or evil, it can make it that much more difficult to recognize the impurity within the "right" side. During the Vietnam War years, I listened to many advocates for social change. As they pointed out evils in the society, they did not seem to want to recognize or deal with their own "evils" within. The picture was painted that our younger generation was all right, whereas the older generation was all wrong. The Apostle Paul says, "Don't get so angry that you sin" (Ephesians 4:26 a CEV). We were angry at social evil, but we overlooked our own sinful reactions to society and other sins in our lives. Each generation seems to fall for this same old human temptation.

Using Good to Deny Evil

The Apostle Paul tells us that the Law of Moses given to the Jews ended up a bad thing (Romans 9:31 ff). It wasn't because the Law was bad; it was that people developed a Pharisee-like attitude when they attempted to follow it. "Look at me. I am 'holier than thou.' You know, I'm not like that sinful person over there. He's a tax collector. And furthermore, when I carry out my act of charity—such as helping a poor widow—make sure that trumpet sounds." Of course, for those of us engaged in helping others, sounding trumpets today would not reach as many people as do newspapers and television. As we work at being moral and doing good deeds, there are other things at work we commonly deny. We are tempted to use that which is good to cover over that which is bad. The Pharisees prided themselves on following the Law, but this led to a self-righteousness which prevented them from seeing their need for a savior. The rich young ruler who came to Jesus probably felt that he wasn't doing so badly (Luke 18:18 ff.). When Jesus asked him about some of the Ten Commandments, he responded that he had been observing them. Indeed, he may have honestly felt that he was conforming to the Ten Commandments. His friends and relatives probably told him, "You're an all right kind of guy." With his stature in the community, no doubt he had developed this "rep." He now came to Jesus asking about eternal life.

Today, such a situation would be the dream of any evangelist—having someone with political power and financial means asking about eternal life. This potential convert even had the reputation of being a good person in the community, one who tried to live by the Ten Commandments.[8] But that reputation seems to have gone to his head.

The rich young ruler evidently wasn't around when Jesus gave the Sermon on the Mount. In that sermon the commandment against murder goes beyond the actual act. The question becomes, have you ever cursed someone in your heart? The test of adultery is, have you ever looked at someone with thoughts of adultery? Neither the rich young ruler nor anyone else could honestly say that he or she had passed such tests. Thus, the rich young ruler's feeling that he was observing God's holy law was a trap. This "goodness" also prevented him from facing the other side of his life: an attachment to wealth and a related insensitivity to the poor.

When I took the job as director of a homeless shelter in 1989, the management of the sponsoring organization was in turmoil. It was a church-affiliated, not-for-profit organization that expanded very rapidly—faster than the staff was able to cope with. The government increased funding to the shelter due to its proven capability of helping people in need. Many of the leaders of the organization invoked this early success to avoid the serious management problems they faced. Most of the staff, working under great stress, were demoralized. The organization's reputation for doing a good work tended to keep it from facing the things that were destroying it. As time went on, these organizational weaknesses inevitably surfaced; it was only then that changes were made. Throughout this process some wanted to recognize only the strengths of the organization, while others dwelt only on the flaws.

The "goodness" of the world has become its snare. It has, in fact, turned into a trap for individuals, for social and ethnic groups, and for nations. We use the bad we find in others to deny any good they may have. And then we use the good found in us or our groups to deny our own evil within. This is humanity's way of resolving the tension of living in a mixed-bag world. People do not want to face up to what happened as a result of humanity's spiritual fall—that we are living an experience of good and evil inseparably bonded together.

Untangling the Knots

The Apostle Paul tells us to "hate everything that is evil and hold tight to everything that is good" (Romans 12:9 CEV). In another epistle Paul says, "Whatever is true, whatever is honorable, whatever is just, whatever is pure, whatever is pleasing, whatever is commendable, if there is any excellence and if there is anything worthy of praise, think about these things" (Philippians 4:8 NRSV). Rather than latching on to solutions that don't work or just resigning ourselves to things as they are, Paul points us to the real hope of the world. Jesus Christ is the answer to the world's experience of good and evil. No longer do we have to accept the mix of good and evil the world presents us. With Jesus Christ, we can begin to untangle the knots of good and evil inseparably bound since humanity's fall.

When Jesus told the story of the good Samaritan, the Jewish listeners were challenged not to simplify and categorize. The Samaritans were scorned by most Jews. In the story, it was a Samaritan who carried out an act that demonstrated love of neighbor while the "religious" Jews did not. The probable knee-jerk reaction of many of the Jewish listeners was to conclude that Jesus was either minimizing doctrine, or worse, advocating the Samaritan view of their doctrinal dispute. And yet, when Jesus speaks with the Samaritan woman at the well, he identifies with the Jewish side of the dispute over the issue of worship; "You Samaritans worship what you do not know; we worship what we do know, for salvation is from the Jews" (John 4:22 NIV). But the woman is not led merely to conform to the current Jewish practice. Jesus goes on to put the entire issue of worship in its proper context; "God is spirit, and his worshipers must worship in spirit and in truth" (John 4:24 NIV).

How can we be liberated from this temptation to simplify problems in extreme black-and-white groupings? To be freed from this pitfall, a supernatural perspective is required whereby our judgment is not clouded by the limitations of our own experience. In the Old Testament, Isaiah tells about the coming Messiah who "will not judge by what he sees with his eyes, or decide by what he hears with his ears" (Isaiah 11:3b NIV). With a perspective rooted in Christ who transcends our own social and cultural limitations, we have the opportunity to make a real change in the world.

God didn't create us as a mixed bag of good and evil. Humans were created in God's own image to reflect the Creator's own pure, loving, and righteous nature. We were to be connected to God and mirror his character in our lives. Yet the good and bad parts are so intertwined that even what seems good is often tainted. People mess up their own goodness when they don't give God the credit for the goodness that exists either in their society or in their own lives. Jesus had to remind the rich young ruler, "No one is good—except God alone" (Luke 18:19b NIV). Scripture compares our righteousness to filthy rags (Isaiah 64:6). Among other things, pride is mixed into what on the surface seems good.

To be an instrument of real change in the world requires that we ourselves change. So often we see a lack of humility among those dedicated to social change because their focus is always on someone else, on the perpetrators of injustice. Yet stories circulate about the abusiveness of many activists. Narrowness of focus on the problems of the world leads to blind spots. During the 1960s, while caught up in the social movements of my time, I neglected other areas of my own life that needed to be changed. Jesus Christ offers healing from the blindness that befalls those engaged in attacking the evils in the world.

In Christ, our righteousness is no longer our own; it is a righteousness that comes from God working within us. Paul tells us in Philippians 3:9, "For now my place is in him, and I am not dependent upon any of the self-achieved righteousness of the Law. God has given me that genuine righteousness which comes from faith in Christ" (PHILLIPS). Not only are we released from guilt, we are also set free to do good works in the world (e.g., Romans 6:18). God is at work removing the pride and the wrong motives which so often accompany our actions.

The uniqueness of Christian social action is our call to be "imitators of God" (Ephesians 5:1 NIV), to live in a Christlike manner. Breaking out of our social and cultural limitations, we recognize God as the source of all good in the world. As such, we take on the quality of being open-minded to wherever good is found in the world. Good is not seen as limited to Christians; some good or some truth can come from a republican or a democrat, a socialist or a capitalist, a Muslim or an atheist. Therefore, we should be able to listen to and reflect on criticisms arising from those with whom we do not generally agree. We recognize that Christians, no matter how dedicated, are not completely free from evil. Our vision can now be expanded because we have given ourselves to "the true light that gives light to every [person]" (John 1:9 NIV). While the image of God in humanity is smeared and distorted because of sin (John Calvin asserts that it has not been completely erased), with Christ that image begins to be restored.

The world's misleading, inaccurate categorizing of good and evil pushes us to accept a tainted package which contrasts with the purity of God's kingdom. We don't need to tolerate or excuse evil in order to identify with a good cause. Because of Christ we can accept the good while opposing the bad. This is the vision needed to sort through our cultural surroundings and have our lifestyles reflect the kingdom of God.

3

CATCHING HUMANITY'S SICKNESS

There is a verse from Paul's letter to the Romans many Christians commit to memory because of its importance. Like John 3:16, this verse is said to be a summary of the Gospel. Paul tells us in Romans 5:6 (NIV), "You see, at just the right time, when we were still powerless, Christ died for the ungodly." The word *powerless* is translated in some versions as *weak* or *helpless*.

What makes us think that people have control over sin? We can all recall times when we changed certain aspects of our lives. We see children receiving discipline and changing bad habits as they grow up. Most people can recall an experience of stopping something they knew was wrong. As a result, we develop this feeling that we possess some degree of power over sin. Consequently, when we hear of a heinous crime, we assume that the perpetrator could have chosen not to do it.

Earlier we noted that the moral good in our lives often becomes a screen for denying the evil that is also present. Likewise, the perception that we have some control over sin reinforces a denial of the hold that sin can have on us. We believe that with effort and willpower we can prevent or reverse sin in our lives. We then project this common assumption on to the events of our world. History shows that many social evils of the past were in fact overcome. The elimination of slavery and colonialism are two examples of the world seemingly changing itself for the better, although it was not a simple process.

Caught in the Web

Let us go back to the first sin mentioned in the Bible. Adam and Eve didn't kill anyone. They did not do some terrifying or horrendous crime which today would appear on the evening news and shock us. All they did was eat something they were not supposed to eat. What's the big deal? Should they not have been excused for that?

But God told them and all of humanity that if you sin, you will die (Genesis 2:17). Paul tells us in Romans 3:23 that "all have sinned and fall short of the glory of God" (NIV). Just because we are not murderers or robbers or prostitutes does not mean that we are free from sin. Envy is identified in the Ten Commandments and everyone would have to admit to this one. Sin is not just a violation of God's law through specific actions, it is also living in separation from God. Sin is living a life lacking in love of God and love of fellow human beings. Before God, everyone is affected by sin. No person who has ever lived on earth, except for Jesus Christ, can claim to be completely free of its power. And so everyone of us is caught up in sin, even when we think we have a degree of control over it.

Paul tells us that this problem confronted the Jewish people in their history. They knew there was a true living God who created the universe. And they knew about God's laws for right living. But it was not enough to know what God wanted them to do. The Old Testament shows the Israelites time and time again straying away from God. They wandered off in spite of God's miracles and self-revelation. They lacked power. They had the knowledge of God but they were limited by their human nature.

Paul was a very religious Jewish leader before he turned to Christ. As a Pharisee, he studied and worked hard at obeying the Old Testament laws. Yet in the final analysis, he could not live out what he knew was right. In Romans chapter 7, Paul has broken through his own denial. He admits this by saying, "In my mind I want to be God's willing servant but instead I find myself still enslaved to sin" (TLB).

Paul admits what everyone should be acknowledging: that our human nature prevents us from living a truly righteous life. We cannot even live up to the ideals that we have set for ourselves, much less those in the Bible. This is the powerlessness Paul speaks about. It seems we have some kind of disease, some kind of sickness that prevents us from doing exactly what God wants us to do. The prophet Jeremiah, seeing the sin of his people, asks, "If medicine and doctors may be found in Gilead, why aren't my people healed?" (Jeremiah 8:22 CEV).

Jesus points to himself as the one who can heal this sin-sickness referred to in the Old Testament (see John 12:40-41). He also tells us that "everyone who sins is a slave to sin" (John 8:34 b NIV). A slave is certainly someone who is powerless over his or her condition. While we may try to avoid thinking of ourselves as helpless in the face of sin, Jesus commands us to recognize this spiritual condition. He makes this statement about slavery and sin to a group of Pharisees who maintain that they are not powerless (John 8:33). Later, after Jesus heals a man who was born blind, he tells those who are not blind that they too are in need of healing (John 9). A group of Pharisees display their denial by responding, "What? Are we blind too?" Jesus answers them, "If you were blind, you would not be guilty of sin; but now that you claim you can see, your guilt remains" (John 9:40-41 NIV). Powerlessness and the need for healing are found in these encounters.

Yet, even though the Bible makes many links between sickness and sin, we must be very careful. People tend to get mixed up on this point. Some take this to mean that Christians can resign themselves to a life of sin and imperfection. "I can't change, it's just sin disease," someone may say when confronted with sinful behavior in his or her life.

The Limits of Human Willpower

In the early 1970s a popular comedian named Flip Wilson starred in a weekly television show. One of the characters he

played was a feisty female character who frequently mis-
behaved. When caught telling a lie, she would say, "The devil
made me do it!" People laughed because this character found an
easy way out of taking responsibility. She insisted that her
wrongdoing wasn't her fault. Do we have any responsibility for
sin or are we only helpless victims?

Many people have a problem comparing sin with sickness.
They feel that the two things should not be associated. Physical
sickness is, after all, something that most of the time we cannot
help. On the other hand, when people lie, steal, or murder, we
tend to feel that they made a choice to do so. It seems
reasonable to assert that those who commit such immoral acts
have control and could refrain from doing so if they wanted to.
But the question arises, exactly how much control do people
really have over sin?

Working in the field of alcoholism treatment helped to give
me a glimpse of what the Bible is saying on this matter. The
mental health profession treats alcoholism as a disease. Unlike
the clients I worked with, I had never been an alcoholic. Before
taking this job working with alcoholics, I had difficulty understanding how alcoholism could be viewed as a disease. Like
many others, I felt that if I could stop drinking altogether for a
period of time, why couldn't the alcoholic do it?

That alcoholics are caught up in something they no longer
have power over was something I learned quickly. A physical
addiction has taken away their power over alcohol. What does
one normally do if one has a disease that is ultimately fatal? The
person goes for treatment. One seeks out help. And that is the

key. It is a healthy sign for people to want to rid themselves of sickness

For the alcoholic, the first step towards recovery is recognizing his or her own powerlessness over alcohol.[1] Paul admitted his own powerlessness over sin and his need for the overcoming power which comes from Christ. Now Paul would give credit to God, not to himself, for whatever good works he accomplished in his life. Paul tells us in Romans 12:1-2 that through God's mercy, we can be released from our conformity to the world, and hence, from our society's entrapment in sin. People can now live by the *mercy of God* rather than live at the *mercy of the world*, their social environment. But most alcoholics do not line up for treatment at the first sign of symptoms. The reason is something called *denial*.

Hiding from Reality

The parallel between the denial one finds with an alcoholic and the denial of humankind towards sin is striking. The alcoholic strains to say "I don't have a problem. I can stop drinking at any time." People also think they can conquer sin in their own power. Before coming to Christ, Paul thought that he could live a righteous life in his own strength and ability. Alcoholism messes up a person's life and is fatal over time. Sin has ruined life on earth and is spiritually lethal to everyone. Sin cuts us off from our most important relationship, our relationship with God. In both the case of alcoholism and the case of sin in general, denial shows itself in many different rationalizations and acts of avoidance. Adam and Eve tried to hide from God in the Garden of Eden. They attempted to conceal their guilt and shift blame when confronted. When God asked them about what they had done, they didn't own up.[2] Humanity has become much more sophisticated since Adam and Eve. We now have cultured ways to hide faults in our lives. We shift blame to parents or to our society as though we shared no personal accountability.

Our social environment has made sin and its denial easy for us. Most of us are as aware of our environment as a fish is aware of water. It is hard to recognize how encompassing it can be. There is an ongoing debate among behavioral scientists about whether one's character is determined by environment, genetic makeup, or free will. What is not disputed is that a social environment has an extremely powerful influence in shaping lives. And so the social environment is a dominant factor keeping us powerless over sin.[3]

The Pull to Conform

Social scientists tell us that as people grow up they are shaped and molded to conform to their culture. We can hardly escape from this as it has such an overwhelming pressure on us. It conditions our thinking, our values, and our reactions to things. Consider the very language in which we think and converse. As children grow up, there is little free choice over the language they learn. As adults we continue to use that language for our personal thoughts, without getting tied up in knots over whether or not it best expresses what we are thinking. It takes a very significant effort to stop using one's language and begin using another when everyone else continues to use the first. Without a social group to reinforce the new language, it is very difficult indeed. The socialization process is similar to computer programming. Even to change one aspect of that "programming" (such as language, in our case) takes a great deal of effort.

Social surroundings exert an enormous pull to draw us into doing things we otherwise might not do. Growing up in an urban neighborhood, one may be pressured to join a gang, to get involved in drugs, or to have a baby while still a young teenager. Some poverty-stricken urban neighborhoods have so many males incarcerated that a young male may even consider serving jail time as an initiation to becoming a *real* man. People experience powerlessness when surrounded by such pressures. The social environment pulls at us regardless of the type of community we live in. And again, that pressure is not merely external but internal as well.

Almost from birth, a person can go through a search to become "somebody." Because of this, we have a desire planted in us to be accepted, to obtain identity and status in our world. This inner desire is combined with the external pressure for us to fit into a group. The normal psychological and sociological process of growing up and the desire to be accepted by others can mold us into "the pattern of the world" (see Romans 12:1 NIV). The individual then considers the group or society as inherently good. While in many ways this socialization process is healthy for people, social sin, along with its denial, is also part of the package.

We rarely take into account that so much of our personal identity is patterned by our society. Paul seems to refer to this a few verses before Romans 12, when he tells us that all people are "shut up" in sin (Romans 11:32 NASB). On our own we cannot escape from the social forces in our lives. But it is not just an external pressure, it is also an internal pull. In seeking the acceptance and approval of people around us, we acquire an inner motivation to conform.

Sin, the state of living alienated from God, becomes accepted as one's social environment. Denial of sin is easy when "everyone is doing it." In recent years, many people have become more aware of institutional racism. Many realize that to be guilty of racial prejudice, one doesn't have to stand out by one's personal prejudices; one may just go along with what is considered normal and socially accepted.[4] Unfortunately, following such unexamined social norms frequently results in racial discrimination.

Institutional Sin

Intelligence Quotient (or I.Q.) tests were changed in the United States when it was brought to light that the examination questions took for granted cultural images unfamiliar to lower-income minority people. Research showed that lower income minorities fared worse on these earlier tests, not as a result of a lack of intelligence, but as a result of their having had less experience in the mainstream white culture. Such tests had been used to determine who would go on to more academically advanced classes or to schools for gifted children. The people writing those original I.Q. tests would probably say that they had no intention of discriminating against anyone; they just designed a test. School officials would assert that they too did not intend any bias. No one stands out guilty, yet prejudice takes place. Racism isn't the only expression of sin that can be institutionalized. There are many other kinds of institutionalized sins embedded in our social groupings. Just playing by the rules and conforming to society results in overlooked sinful behavior. No one is responsible, yet the sin is accomplished.

With institutional sin, it is easy to deny personal responsibility. In his call for spiritual revival, John Dawson contends that "the greatest wounds in human history, the greatest injustices, have not happened through the acts of some individual perpetrator; rather through the institutions, systems, philosophies, cultures, religions, and governments of *humankind*. Because of this, we, as individuals, are tempted to absolve ourselves of all individual responsibility." He goes on to say that "unless somebody identifies themselves with corporate entities, such as the nation of our citizenship, or the subculture of our ancestors, the act of honest confession will never take place."[5] Dawson sees the failure of people to own up and confess participation in corporate sins, such as racism, to be a major obstacle in the way of real revival. We need to acknowledge how our conformity has engulfed us in institutional sin.

Going Against the Grain

Escaping group conformity is difficult because of the negative consequences awaiting those who do not conform. A person may be shunned as an outcast, be denied economic rights and privileges, or even be subject to arrest and repression by government authorities. The more a particular group or society barricades itself against outside views, the more forceful its reaction to dissent becomes. Although someone may identify with the group's overall values and culture, loyalty to the group may be questioned when too much independent thinking is displayed. Group conformity is maintained in various ways. The socialization process, assumed values, and forceful pressure on those who deviate all contribute to keeping people in line.

The theologian Reinhold Niebuhr points out another way we are kept from questioning our social groups. In his classic work, *Moral Man and Immoral Society*, he details a way used by people to maintain denial towards social evil. According to Niebuhr, individuals want to believe that their group could never carry out something they themselves find morally unacceptable on an individual level. As a result, people tend to romanticize and obscure the truth regarding evils perpetuated by their society.[6] The powerlessness to resist conformity stems from multiple external and internal factors.

We see this social conformity at work in the pressures we experience to live materialistically, to the point of spending beyond our means.[7] Then there is the ease by which we can join a group in demeaning certain other people. When we find ourselves encircled by prejudiced people, it is difficult to buck the tide and act in a non-biased manner. The social environment makes it easy to sin when we are surrounded all the time by people doing it as part of "normal" everyday life.

Sierra Leone is among the poorer countries of the world. While serving there as a missionary, I was confronted by the materialism which I had taken for granted as someone raised in the United States. It was difficult for me to grasp this fully at first. My own parents had struggled over the years to pull themselves out of poverty. I was the first to graduate from college in my family. At the time, my parents did not even have the means to contribute towards my college costs. Consequently, I had never thought of myself as well off. However, while in Sierra Leone I realized that I was more materialistic than most people around me. During my stay, I was repeatedly confronted by my own unrecognized materialism. And when I returned home, I experienced a second "culture shock" as I encountered American consumerism again. My wife and I tried to resist becoming recaptured by materialism as we adjusted to life back in the United States, but found that our sensitivity was reduced over time. The pressures of our cultural surroundings proved very difficult to resist.

Our attitudes towards the groups to which we belong fuel this conformity to institutional sin. Do we have a viewpoint outside of our group by which its actions can be judged? Let us bear in mind that a person's god is whatever that person is uncritical of. If one does not have standards to evaluate a particular social group, then that group serves as a "god" for that person. It is an absolute authority in the person's life. The "renewing of our minds" that Paul speaks of in Romans 12:2 includes having a new and different perspective towards our various associations. Christians are called to take on the mind of Christ. Our groups are then evaluated by biblical standards. With renewed minds we can now display behavior that is living proof of "what God's will is—his good, pleasing and perfect will" (NIV). Too many Christians have not been challenged to break their captivity to their social class or racial and ethnic group.[8] They have not yet been challenged to sort out the evil and the good within the groups with which they identify.

A Christ-Like Response

Once we become aware of institutional sin, do we now go out and condemn those who are thoughtlessly caught up in it? That can be an easy temptation, especially if we join with others who share the same feelings. Rather, as Christians, we should seek to take on the same love towards the crowd that Jesus had. Matthew 9:36 reveals the attitude of Jesus towards the crowd: "When he saw the crowds, he had compassion on them, because they were harassed and helpless" (NIV). There is no condemnation, only compassion. Jesus has compassion for our cities and urban neighborhoods which some churches feel should be abandoned. And he has compassion for those caught up in institutional racism and other sins. He sees people as harassed, helpless, and powerless. On the cross, Jesus prays: "Father, forgive them, for they do not know what they are doing" (Luke 23:34 NIV). We should recognize that our world is largely unaware of its sinful activity. We are spiritually blind and can't see the extent of our failings with respect to God, other people, and ourselves. Human beings "do not know what they are doing." But the world is not in a hopeless state. The gospel offers hope and life-changing power to our harassed and helpless world.

People are not so taken in that they cannot see any faults at all within their own society. Certain problems are recognized, yet there is a widespread belief that these problems can be fixed without seeking power and direction from Christ. And those trying to change society often try to do so with blind spots. Sin has so thoroughly permeated human life that many times when we endeavor to treat its different symptoms, our "solutions" end up creating new problems.

We must not accept the humanistic philosophy of putting faith in humankind's ability *alone* to change individuals and the world for the better. Then we exclude God. Our modern world is saturated with this kind of secular humanism; it's also a problem for many of those engaged in social action. Many of us get caught up in "institutionalized secular humanism."[9] Whereas we Christians often do not practice what we preach, many millions of people actively practice this kind of secular humanism although they may not preach it at all.

History gives repeated examples of groups who shake off one evil in their society only to bring about something worse. This problem has applied to many cult groups that start out by rejecting some of the evils of the world. We have seen this also at work with Communism and with other movements promising to end the problems of society. As dictatorial Communism diminishes in the world, the ugly face of ethnic violence arises in its place. In Russia, following the fall of Communism, many former KGB thugs have become the "muscle" for newly organized crime organizations. History shows that more often than not, people rise up and resist conformity to one defective social system only to attach themselves to another flawed system.

In Luke 11:24-26 (NIV), Jesus tells us that "when an evil spirit comes out of a man, it goes through arid places seeking rest and does not find it. Then it says, 'I will return to the house I left.' When it arrives, it finds the house swept clean and put in order. Then it goes and takes seven other spirits more wicked than itself, and they go in and live there. And the final condition of that man is worse than the first." It is not enough just to be a non-conformist rejecting particular values of society. The transformation Paul speaks about in Romans 12:2 is also needed. We do not need to replace one kind of evil with another kind of evil.

The Heavenly Kingdom

Many of us are confused by Jesus' words to Pontius Pilate: "My kingdom is not of this world" (John 18:36 NIV). People have misunderstood this to mean that Jesus was talking only about heaven in the bye and bye; the kingdom is only for our future hope. Although this future hope is part of it, Jesus was also saying that there is nothing in the world *like* the kingdom of God. While I was growing up, we would say about something very special, "it's out of this world!" We meant that, compared to anything else we had known before, this other thing was completely new and so much better. The kingdom of God is so unique, so utterly different from what people are used to that when they see it demonstrated, they can't figure out its source. This is because its source is *not of this world*. The source is of heaven.

Christians involved in social action often have a problem with focusing on heaven. They may have had experiences with those "so heavenly minded that they are of no earthly good." Some people say that adopting an other-worldly Christianity prevented the slaves in America from challenging the status quo. To avoid this passivity, they maintain, one needs to be more earthly minded in order to be of more earthly good.

The Christian lifestyle should reflect heaven here on earth. In Colossians 3:2, Paul says, "Set your minds on things above, not on earthly things" (NIV). People may one day set up a colony on the moon or on Mars, but Christians are to be a colony of heaven set up on earth. In heaven there is love, there is peace, there is justice and righteousness. Heaven is a place filled with closeness to God, with worship of the Father, Son, and Holy Spirit. Because of this commitment to the things of heaven, we can no longer tolerate the injustice, oppression, violence, and other evils accepted as natural to life here on earth. Christians are a heavenly counter-culture.

This kind of attachment to heaven gave black slaves a foundation for resisting the degradation of slavery. A number of scholars have gone back to the spiritual songs of the slaves and discovered that unlike what many people think, heaven wasn't just some escape from reality. Slaves would sing, "I've got shoes, you've got shoes, All of God's children got shoes. When I get to heaven goin' to put on my shoes, Goin' to walk all over God's heaven." It wasn't something they had to wait for in the future; they had shoes as they sang. According to James Cone, heaven wasn't merely a distant hope for the slaves, but rather "an experience of freedom that has already broken into their present." It enabled them "to know that the existing state of oppression contradicts their real humanity as defined by God's future."[10] It was their basis for challenging the evil they experienced on earth.

The power of the Holy Spirit is needed in order to adopt a truly transformed lifestyle in the world. There is a way to break out of our captivity to one social group or another. Jesus Christ offers strength in place of the powerlessness resulting from societal pressure. People can rise above being mere products of their social environment. As Dr. Martin Luther King Jr. once said, "Only through an inner spiritual transformation do we gain the strength to fight vigorously the evils of the world in a humble and loving spirit."[11] While many different religions in the world talk about doing good, Christianity is distinguished in that Jesus Christ offers people real *power* for living a new life. Because of Someone not bound by any of the world's systems, we are liberated from the slavery to conform. We now have freedom to live for God's kingdom which is "not of this world." We now can be rescued not only from the hold of institutional racism, but from other institutionalized sins as well. Christ alone brings us out of conformity to our social group to transformation in God's new order, the kingdom of God. Real radical change is made in the world when God's will is done on earth as it is in heaven.

4

FROM CONFORMITY TO "TRANSFORMITY"

In 1994 the world was shocked as hundreds of thousands of people became victims of genocidal murder in Rwanda. A long-standing conflict between the two large ethnic groups comprising this African nation erupted into violence. As civil war engulfed the country, the president died in a mysterious plane crash. Shortly afterwards, people in the Hutu majority, who had controlled the country, began attacking and murdering those of the Tutsi minority. Whole families and even entire villages were massacred. The Hutu mobs engaging in these ruthless acts compelled other Hutu to join in.

As the horrors of Rwanda captivated the world's attention, the question came to mind: what of the Christian influence? A large number of churches existed in Rwanda, and many

Rwandans identified themselves as Christian. What was happening with Rwandan Christians while these massacres took place? As journalists pieced together the events, they found that many religious leaders were also pushed into participating in these attacks. A newspaper article quoted one Hutu pastor as saying, "Everyone had to participate." He went on to say that "being a pastor was not an excuse. They said you can have religion afterwards."[1] As a result, he joined in with the mobs but claimed that he didn't actually kill anyone himself.

Here again, in the face of a clear-cut social evil, Christians were pressured to conform. The words of that pastor parallel the response of most German Christians to the Nazis, and the response of most white American Christians to slavery and segregation. Large numbers of Christians in these situations simply conform to social evil. If so many Christians have difficulty resisting the prevailing currents in these extraordinary circumstances, what happens when the social evil is not as blatant? To what degree should Christians resist their culture, particularly if much good as well as evil can be found within it?

In the past few decades, many African Christian leaders and theologians have struggled intensely with the question of how to relate Christianity to traditional African culture. Most Western missionaries in Africa over the past two hundred years viewed traditional African culture as unchristian and uncivilized. When people there accepted the faith, they were taught to disdain such cultural expressions as traditional music and dance styles. These were considered pagan practices. As a result, African Christians were compelled to adopt Euro-

American music and worship styles.[2] When the independence movement swept through the African continent in the 1950s and the 1960s, many African Christian leaders came forward to challenge this view. Today one finds creative expressions of the Christian faith throughout Africa within the context of authentic African culture.

While in Sierra Leone, I was greatly inspired to see how Christians were connected to their traditional culture. But a few of the practices adopted by some independent churches appeared to be conformity rather than cultural transformation. Some independent churches, for example, incorporated animal sacrifices and the use of charms to counteract evil spells. Many African Christians recognize the flaw of Western Christians confusing Christianity with Western culture. The question African Christians face is, How do they escape the temptation of conformity to their own culture? This question is particularly urgent given the pressures experienced by Christians within Rwanda to comply with the social evil taking place there.

Moving from conformity towards transformation or "transformity" is a challenge for Christians in every culture.[3] Not only in Africa but throughout the world, many Christians have come to question the dominance of Western Euro-American culture. African-Americans and other ethnic minorities in the United States have had to address misrepresentations of Jesus as a blond, blue-eyed Caucasian. Christian materials published for widespread use showed little sensitivity to other cultural experiences. But African-American Christians and other minorities are not immune to the pressure to conform. In some cases this can be simply to a particular style of worship or a way of "having church." Some can be so locked into a pattern of an earlier era that they are incapable of visualizing how contemporary culture can be transformed. Years ago, many African-American Christians resisted the use of gospel music because it incorporated rhythms of the urban nightlife. In recent years the challenge is to transform the reality of newer generations, for example, contemporary jazz and hip-hop. All types of cultures, even urban street culture, can in some way be transformed.[4] One should also see culture as much more than just music and artistic style. How do we transform our worlds of work, school, family life, and other social involvements?

Relearning Culture

"Don't let the world around you squeeze you into its own mould, but let God re-mould your minds from within, so that you may prove in practice that the plan of God for you is good, meets all his demands and moves toward the goal of true maturity" (Romans 12:2 PHILLIPS). Many other translations use the phrases "do not be conformed" and "be transformed." When Christians do not stop to examine their culture (i.e., their "world"), they generally fall into the trap of mere conformity. In this verse we see that transformation involves both a relearning (the remolding of our minds) and a corresponding demonstration (the proving in practice). Jesus says that a person must become as a child when he or she enters the kingdom of God (see Matthew 18:2–6). When reflecting on these words, people generally neglect one characteristic of children: that children go through the process of learning their culture. Therefore, after being born again as a child of God, one needs to go through the socialization process of learning the ways of God's kingdom. Christians need to relearn from the perspective of God's kingdom what they have learned as children. Christians are *born again* and this is followed by their *learning again*. This means allowing God to reshape all of the culture instilled in us (much of which is uncritically accepted) going back to when we were children.

Paul goes on in Romans chapter 12 to explain some of the relearning involved as people move from conformity to transformation. He outlines the new kinds of thinking and practices which contrast with the "normal" patterns of the world. One set of traits mentioned has to do with the human ego. In most societies, people are encouraged to get ahead, to seek after admiration and praise, to do things in order to be awarded social recognition. We get added status as we do things which are highly regarded by our particular society and social group. This, in turn, feeds our egos. People can become so drunk with their own egos that they cannot think straight. Paul says Christians must think of themselves soberly. We are now to take on a humility which allows us to confess our weaknesses and shortcomings instead of concealing them. With a new identity in Christ, we can now have healthy self-relationships not dependent merely on social approval. The destructive acts resulting from a poor self-image occur not only in impoverished communities, but everywhere.

Paul goes on to describe the way our relationship patterns move from conformity to transformation (Romans 12:4 ff.). God brings together people from social groups normally separated from one another. In every society we find people who are discriminated against or oppressed by others. In God's new order, people of different ethnic backgrounds and classes begin to come together in love. Normal social conformity means growing up to perpetuate cycles of hate and discrimination. *Transformity* means thinking and acting differently towards those the society considers "outsiders." This also applies to the way in which Christians treat those who wrong them. Unlike the common social response, Paul says, "Do not repay anyone evil for evil. Be careful to do what is right in the eyes of everybody. If it is possible, as far as it depends on you, live at peace with everyone" (Romans 12:17–18 NIV). This teaching parallels the words of Jesus in the Sermon on the Mount regarding enemies (see Matthew 5:44–48). By showing love to those they have been conditioned by their society to scorn, Christians break with worldly conformity.

Transformation requires a rethinking of what we tend to take so much for granted within our cultures. Allowing God to remold us from within involves praying for the power of the Holy Spirit to change us. This change causes us to stop justifying our conformity to the pattern of the world, otherwise known as "worldliness." I noted in the first chapter that the power of worldly society to keep people in line revolves around the rewards Satan offered to Christ in the wilderness. These can be summed up as money, political power, and status. These things can distort not only the Church, but anyone starting out with good intentions. Conformity and worldliness are perpetuated as people become ensnared by money, power, and social status.

The Means and the Ends

Many people living in affluent nations have fallen into the trap of confusing "the means" and "the ends." Jacques Ellul has drawn attention to this problem. He also applies this insight to Christians involved in social concern. Both as social scientist and as theologian, Ellul explains how modern Western society has lost its focus on higher purposes by turning what should be only the means into the ends itself. In his classic book, *The Technological Society*, he shows that the frantic endeavors of modern Western society are geared mainly towards the purpose of producing better means.[5] As our society loses sight of higher ends, the means then become the ends.

People experience this on an individual level. We may hear people say they consider a car to be simply a means to get to work. Yet many people work hard to spend their paychecks on buying and maintaining their cars. Some even send out résumés to compete for better jobs so they can acquire a luxury automobile. Their driving will still be primarily to get them to and from work. And many people work hard so they can buy fashionable clothes to wear on their jobs or to job-related events. Others attend classes in the evening to get another degree so they can advance themselves on their jobs. Once they receive an advancement, they are then expected to have a more expensive lifestyle to match up to their higher salary. After that, they experience social pressure to own a house and take vacations overseas. Soon, they are considering taking on a second job or a second mortgage in order to keep up with the expectations of their new lifestyle (while complaining about the high cost of living). Society pushes us to make a living, but it does not say what it is all for in the end.

What are the end purposes of our living in society? How can we Christians transform our activities so they will serve the purposes of God's kingdom? Someone once came up to Jesus and asked, "Which is the greatest commandment?" In other words, "What purposes should my life serve?" In Matthew 22:36, Jesus answers him, " 'Love the Lord your God with all your heart and with all your soul and with all your mind. . . .' And the second is like it: 'Love your neighbor as yourself.' " (Matthew 22:37, 39 NIV). Humanity was created to serve the purposes of loving God, neighbor, and self.

Jesus Christ came into the world to restore the broken relationships resulting from sin. He knew his mission and purpose in the world. Jesus understood the end purposes he was to reach—to rescue humanity from sin and death, to restore the world as a place of love. Yet Satan wasn't going to sit back while Jesus restored what he had ruined. But how could he tempt Christ? In the wilderness, Satan didn't try to alter the purposes of Jesus' mission, but to go after the means Jesus would use. This is the trap many Christians fall into after they become preoccupied with social ills.

How many times do we see people in the right go astray because of the means they employ? We all know the expression, "the ends justify the means." But this kind of thinking is destructive. Some people say that if you have a good goal in mind, then you can use any means necessary to reach that end. In movies we see "heroes" committing immoral acts to achieve their higher goals. We are encouraged to excuse them because they are battling a greater evil. Throughout the world we find people appealing to this same logic. Lethal force and even terrorism are justified by groups fighting for what they consider to be a worthy cause. Communism failed because many people realized that violently oppressive dictatorship was not just a temporary means used for economic liberation; rather, it had in fact become the ongoing modus operandi of the so-called liberated society. For so many acts of violence around the world, we hear the declaration that they are necessary to achieve a good and just cause. We find other kinds of sinful acts in addition to violence justified in the name of some worthy end.

Money, Power, and Status

Satan tempted Christ by offering him a set of means purporting to accomplish the ends that Jesus sought.[6] These means are also the things which people are tempted to run after as ends in themselves. In Luke 4, we find Jesus fasting in the wilderness at the beginning of his ministry. After completing forty days of fasting, Jesus was hungry. He knew the pangs of hunger. And so Satan tempted him, "If you are the Son of God, command this stone to become a loaf of bread." Jesus gave him this response: "It is written, 'One does not live by bread alone' " (Luke 4:3–4 NRSV). The devil says in effect, "Jesus, you need food, clothing, and shelter; you need money and finances for what you want to accomplish. How are you going to be successful without such things? Jesus, let *me* show you how to get what you need to accomplish these ends."

The interesting thing is that there is nothing sinful about wanting food, shelter, and clothing. Everyone needs these things. But the world is caught up in chasing after these means as ends in themselves. In the United States and in many other societies, people are caught up in consumerism. We are led to believe that material things will somehow make us secure and happy for life. In his response to Satan, Jesus puts material things in their right perspective.[7]

The Apostle Paul tells us in Romans 1:17, "The righteous will live by faith" (NIV). Life is not about striving for material things. It is about a trusting relationship with the God who created us. In the Sermon on the Mount, Jesus says, "Don't worry and ask yourselves, 'Will we have anything to eat? Will we have anything to drink? Will we have any clothes to wear?' Only people who don't know God are always worrying about such things. Your Father in heaven knows that you need all of these" (Matthew 6:31–32 CEV). And then Jesus follows with these great words, "But seek first his kingdom and his righteousness, and all these things will be given to you as well" (Matthew 6:33 NIV).

The world is obsessed with pursuing the means of survival as the ends of life. Material things have become objects of worship and veneration for many. Our culture is saturated with messages telling us that the material-filled life is "the good life."

Many Christians are caught up in the pursuit of wealth. Yet, like an addicted person in denial, when confronted about materialism we say, "I can give it up at any time." Western-world Christians especially need to have anxiety over material things replaced by faith in God, who will provide for our real needs.[8] By living out our faith in this way, we move away from worldly conformity.

The issue of worship comes up again in the second temptation Satan throws at Jesus. "The devil led him up to a high place and showed him in an instant all the kingdoms of the world. And he said to him, 'I will give you all their authority and splendor, for it has been given to me, and I can give it to anyone I want to. So if you worship me, it will all be yours'" (Luke 4:5–7 NIV). Here, Jesus is tempted by political power as a means to accomplish his mission. Satan says in effect, "Look, Jesus, can't you see how much more effective you will be if you were crowned Emperor, not only of the Roman Empire but of all the kingdoms of the world? How much more could you accomplish with all that power at your fingertips. You would be able to straighten out the world and all the mess it's in."

Political power has always been a temptation for humanity. Political power carries with it a sense of awe, almost a quality of worship.[9] Having once tasted political power, it's very hard for many people to give it up. Political leaders can make decisions that alter history. Yet, like money, political power easily becomes an end in itself. Throughout the world we find people fighting and killing each other over political power. Although democratic countries like the United States have checks and balances to curb the concentration of power, we still find the thirst for political power bringing out the worst in people. Through this temptation, Satan presents an attractive deal. But there is a little catch. As with some of our modern contracts, we find some hard-to-read small print at the bottom of the page. Andy Rooney of the *60 Minutes* television program once said, "Nothing in fine print is ever good news." The subtle "fine print" found here is "If you will worship, it will all be yours."

Throughout the ages, Christians have been tempted by political power. But so often there is a catch, a price that has to be paid for this political power. Many times it is giving up some of the worship normally reserved for God and giving it instead to some political system or political leader. At other times, we allow our political involvement to fall outside of God's control. Political power then operates as an autonomous force, not subjected to God. Jesus gives his answer: "It is written: 'Worship the Lord your God and serve him only'" (Luke 4:8 NIV).

Satan now puts one last temptation before Christ. "Throw yourself down" from the highest point of the temple (Luke 4:9). It seems that the appeal of what is now being offered is social status. For one to jump off the temple and land safely would be a public relations bonanza. Doing this would make anyone an instant celebrity with name recognition. He or she would command public attention similar to that of a movie star or sports superstar. The devil approaches Jesus like a high-priced public relations consultant, suggesting the perfect publicity stunt. The boost in ratings would be immediate. But Jesus turns down this temptation of social status as he rejects the temptations of economic and political power. We can imagine Satan saying, "Jesus, how in the world are you going to get this kingdom program off the ground? You don't have financial backing. You don't have political connections. You can't even get your name in *People* magazine." Continuing to plead his case, Satan might say, "I know all about this world. I know what it takes to get ahead in the world. People run after what will get them their next meal. They are impressed by political power and celebrities. You won't get far without these things." After Jesus resisted these temptations, the Bible says that the devil "left him until an opportune time" (Luke 4:13).

An Opportune Time for Tempting

That opportune time is the week known as "Holy Week," beginning on Palm Sunday. The setting for the tempting is Jerusalem. During Holy Week, two kinds of kingdoms clash. The kingdoms of the world are intoxicated with money, power, and status, while God's kingdom focuses instead on faith, hope, and love.

Jesus enters Jerusalem without any money to speak of. How does one keep a movement going without finances? That question was apparently of much concern to Judas, the treasurer of the group. Here we have Judas put in charge of a bank that was almost always empty. No matter that each time there was a need for something—such as feeding a crowd of five thousand—somehow there was always enough to go around. The trust that "God will provide" was not something Judas was able to put in his bank. The thirty pieces of silver offered Judas was a real temptation. We can almost hear the devil telling Jesus, "Look at your followers living in poverty. Hey, Jesus, if you would only give some perks to your disciples—a chariot made by Lexus, a luxury townhouse in Jerusalem—maybe they wouldn't turn against you."

I visited many churches while in Sierra Leone. One church stood out because it was so alive spiritually. It was a very fast growing church, yet they had no plans to build a parking lot. In fact, you had to walk to the church as there were no roads in that area. The church building was a shack without electricity. It was a borrowed shelter which the church didn't even own. The church members were poor and illiterate. Although I did not understand most of the local language, I certainly felt the presence of Jesus in that place. I encountered such a strong sense of love that I felt I had experienced a little of heaven on earth. The memory of their rich worship and closeness to God has remained with me after these many years. Back in the United States I have seen many churches lacking in such spirituality and love, yet caught up in the myth that if a church makes lots of money it is successful.

The temptation of political power is at work when Jesus is arrested and brought before the political authorities. At his arrest we see Peter and the disciples faltering as they are tempted into responding with violence. One disciple pulls his sword and strikes at the ear of one of those trying to arrest Jesus. We can imagine the idea of an armed revolt to bring Jesus into power flashing in the minds of the disciples. At this moment, Satan's political offer is extremely attractive. The disciples themselves are even falling for it. Jesus rejects it again as he says, "Put your sword away. . . . Don't you know that I could ask my Father, and right away he would send me more than twelve armies of angels?" (Matthew 26:52–53 CEV). Jesus continues to reject this lure of political power during his interrogations by Pilate and Herod.

The Church is tempted to become enamored with political power and, subsequently, to lose perspective. There is the tendency to support the status quo with the powers that be or, particularly for those committed to social change, to put great faith in political power as a solution for eradicating social evil. Jacques Ellul describes this as submitting to a "political illusion." Many of us have been quick to wed ourselves to a particular political philosophy. Political leaders and movements come and go, whereas the kingdom of God is eternal. Someone has observed that the church that marries itself to the spirit of the age is like a man who marries and is soon left a widower. Our political involvement should be guided by the principles of God's eternal kingdom.

The competition between the desire for social popularity and the focus of God's kingdom on love is also evident during Holy Week. The temptation of popularity heats up as the crowds fill Jerusalem for Passover. Having the ability to impress a crowd, having celebrity status, and being in the limelight is a very alluring role. We want to be crowd pleasers. The last thing anyone would want is to be identified as a scorned outcast.

The crowd gives their approval to Jesus on Palm Sunday. A few days later they shout for his death. A few choice words can turn a crowd into a mob. It didn't take the Jewish leaders much effort to turn the crowd against Jesus. As the crowd shouts, "Crucify him," we can imagine Satan suggesting again that last temptation offered in the wilderness. "Jesus, this is the right time and place. Now is the time to go up to the highest point in the temple, jump, and land safely in front of everyone. Or maybe you can wait and jump down off the cross. You'll have the crowd back on your side again. They'll be praising you like they did on Palm Sunday."

A news report I ran aross in 1994 noted that compensation was being paid to African-Americans who had lived in a Florida town seventy years before. At that time, a white woman claimed she had been assaulted by a black man. A mob of whites quickly gathered and went to the African-American town. For the next four days they attacked every black man, woman, and child they could get their hands on. Innocent people were massacred. Many others were injured. The mob burned down every house belonging to a black family. People fled for their lives. Some children survived by hiding in the nearby swamps without clothes on their backs. At the time no one questioned whether the claim of that white woman was really true. It is easy to join a crowd in hating someone or some group.

Following the crowd is especially what conformity to the world is about. When people become part of God's kingdom, their relationships with others should no longer be based primarily on social approval and popularity. Rather, love becomes the paramount focus, even when it means the possibility of social opposition. Jesus rejected the trap of going the way of money, power, and social status. He chose instead obedience to God and the way of love. That led to the cross.

A Kingdom of Faith, Hope, and Love

Paul writes, "God demonstrates his own love for us in this: While we were still sinners, Christ died for us" (Romans 5:8 NIV). In Romans 6, he tells us that because of the resurrection of Christ, we can now live a new life. He says that we are now "dead to sin but alive to God" (Romans 6:11 NIV). He adds that because "you have been set free from sin and have become slaves to God, the benefit you reap leads to holiness, and the result is eternal life" (Romans 6:22 NIV). It is by the mercy of God that Christians are drawn out of the worldliness that otherwise keeps us conformed to the way of money, power, and status.

In contrast to this worldliness, God's kingdom is not of this world. It centers on faith, hope, and love. Culture is transformed as Christians live out values based on this eternal kingdom. This does not mean that we are to separate ourselves from society and go off to live in some isolated community. It does mean, however, that we are to separate ourselves from money, status, and power, either as ends in themselves or as gods we must bow to in order to get things done.[10] Satan's desire is for people to get caught up in this kind of worldliness even when they believe that they are pursuing worthy goals. For a Christian, the ends of God's kingdom are to be reflected always in the means which we employ.

C. S. Lewis once said that if something is not eternal then it is eternally out-of-date. Christians are called to model the lifestyle of heaven in contrast to the surrounding worldliness. This is a lifestyle of love, mercy, righteousness, holiness, and closeness to God. This is the transformation resulting from the inner workings of God's Holy Spirit.

A great example of what is meant by transformation can be seen in the life of St. Augustine. Here we find a Roman orator, deeply versed in the history, culture, and philosophy of Roman civilization. Yet when he became a Christian, he put all of that background into the service of God. In his book, *City of God*, he presented and defended Christian truth to other Roman philosophers in terms they could understand. His influence contributed greatly to the infusion of biblical principles into Roman life and culture.[11] All Christians have this charge of moving from conformity to transformity.

"These people are turning the world upside down," people complained of the early Church. What is the secret? "The secret is simply this," Paul says in Colossians 1:27: "Christ *in you!*" (PHILLIPS) It is a secret that, once known, is very hard to keep from others. "So, naturally, we proclaim Christ!" Paul continues, "We warn everyone we meet, and we teach everyone we can, all that we know about him, so that, if possible, we may bring every [person] up to his [or her] full maturity in Christ Jesus" (Colossians 1:28 PHILLIPS). In Christ we grow in faith, hope, and love. This growing process also drives us to sift through our ingrained culture, turning from conformity to transformity.

5

ORGANIC FAITH

A number of years ago, I listened as a Muslim leader explained why Islam was better than Christianity. "Christianity is a system of beliefs," he declared, "while Islam is a *way of living*." This was obviously a simplistic argument, yet one which is very telling about how people around the world— including many Christians—perceive Christianity. While biblical Christianity is also about a way of living, the lack of such practice has sent people looking elsewhere for answers. As Ron Sider notes, "We have not lived what we preached. In disgust, many intellectuals have turned away from our hypocritical Christianity."[1]

Many people have taken issue with Western Christianity because of its historically weak social witness. Such is the case with African-American Christians. They are saddled with the legacies of slavery and segregation as they respond to the challenge of Black Muslims and other movements in their communities. Christians within other minority groups in the United States—including Native Americans, Mexican-Americans, and Asian-Americans—also have much explaining to do in the face of the historical record. These concerns are not limited to the United States. Christian thinkers and theologians in Latin America, Africa, and Asia—places where churches are today growing the fastest—find that they too have to account for the legacy of colonialism and the complicity of Euro-American Christianity in economic exploitation and cultural imperialism. Christians from poorer, oppressed groups and nations struggle to explain the apparent dichotomy between creed and deed in Western Christianity as they present the claims of Jesus Christ to their own cultures.

Even for Western-world Christians looking at their own internal history, it is difficult to account for inconsistencies such as the weak response of the German church to the rise of Hitler. Nazism took hold within a nation recognized for its great contribution to Western culture's philosophical and theological thought. Yet, for the most part, the German churches accommodated themselves to Hitler. Psychiatrist and author M. Scott Peck writes in *Further Along the Road Less Traveled* about how he had to take upon himself "the burden of the sins of the Christian church" when he converted to Christianity a few years before. He points to the church's failure to stop the Holocaust as one of those burdens. He is convinced that "had the Christian churches—as they should have—declared Nazism to be incompatible with Christianity, labeled it worse than heresy and threatened all Nazis with excommunication, the course of history would have been very different."[2]

While many may be unaware of such history, most people are aware of the common separation between Sunday morning and the rest of the week. One doesn't need a degree in the social sciences to see that there is an inconsistency between the "Christian" label given European and North American nations and the secularism, consumerism, and other influences characterizing day-to-day living. And with so many Christians conformed to this social environment, Jacques Ellul pointedly says, "We have to admit that there is an immeasurable distance between all that we read in the Bible and the practice of the church and of Christians."[3] He calls this a perversion or a subversion of Christianity.

While acknowledging many great contributions by Christians in Europe and America, Christian thinkers from Latin America, Africa, and Asia (referred to by many as "the South") have called attention to a problem somewhat unique to Western Christianity. They point to earlier Greek-Hellenistic influences as contributing to Western Christianity's poor social witness. As we noted earlier, people normally do not examine their cultural influences. There is a need to stand back and look at how faith is viewed in the minds of people in the Western world.

As Christians, we inevitably interact with our surrounding culture. Christian commitment may move people to sift through and challenge their culture. Here Christians uphold the positive aspects of their culture while seeking to change the negative aspects.[4] On the other hand, people may try to accom-modate Christianity to a particular culture, supporting whatev-er that culture values and opposing what it rejects. Theologians generally refer to such accommodation as *syncretism*. Although syncretism is in general viewed negatively by Christian theolo-gians, churches have tended to succumb in practice to the temptation of cultural accommodation through the ages. We may be quick to point out cases of syncretism found in the emerging churches of Africa, Asia, and Latin America but have difficulty recognizing it in our own situations. Syncretism is the "beam" that is easier for us to spot in Christians of another culture.[5]

To discern the strengths and weaknesses of our own culture, we need help from others outside our culture. It is important to consider the question raised by those outside of the mainstream of Western society: Does the very definition of biblical faith tend to lose something as it is translated into Western culture?

The Mind Approach of Western Culture

If the distinctive character of Western culture could be captured in a single phrase, it would probably be Descartes' *cogito ergo sum*, i.e., "I think, therefore I am." Western culture distin-guishes itself by its philosophical and intellectual orientation. Cerebral thought and science are major characteristics of Euro-American society. People generally approach reality on an intel-lectual mind level.

Most other worldviews and cultures do not have this type of concern with abstract ideas and intellectualism. This particular orientation of Western society can be traced back to Greek-Hellenistic culture. The ancient Greeks were very concerned with "knowledge" as detached, impersonal, purely intellectual understanding. We find evidence of this in Plato's *Republic*, where the philosophers are on the highest level of society. Although philosophy as a specialized academic discipline does not exert such an influence on Western society, the "mind" approach to life does pervade all aspects of its culture. This mind approach has not only driven science and technology, but it has also influenced theological study.

Too abstract for most churchgoers, the main use of theologians' works is in seminaries as tools for training pastors. But the seminarians can find it difficult relating their book-oriented studies to the practical realities of parish work. Translating the whys and wherefores of theological thinking into the nuts and bolts of the spiritual journey for the average person in the pew is a near-insurmountable task. There *are* ideas and information the theologians present that help us understand the Christian walk, yet their relative inaccessibilty leaves them virtually undiscovered.

Within the history of Western Christianity, theological thought has been greatly influenced by philosophical trends.[6] For example, modern philosophical currents tend to rationalize away supernatural reality, and many theologians follow suit. Beginning with Thomas Aquinas, theologians have come to rely heavily on philosophical arguments to substantiate Christian truth. It is as though the discipline of theology has been taken through a kind of philosophical grinder. As a result, theology has responded by adjustment or reaction, all the while taking on more of a philosophical complexion in the process.[7]

While Christians should neither turn off their intellect nor suspend philosophical considerations, we need to focus our theology on much more than just answering intellectual arguments. What is very pressing is the need to examine the social influences that have shaped our worldviews and behavior, for the most part unconsciously. Among other things, the mind orientation of Western culture needs to be looked at. The overpowering influence of this cultural environment has resulted in people thinking of Christian faith only in terms of "belief." It is taken for granted that Christian "faith" means holding a certain set of intellectual beliefs. But is this a true reading of Christian faith—the faith of the Scriptures?

It is commonly assumed that people move from their beliefs to corresponding actions. Matching actions come second. When we say that a person must first have faith (i.e. belief) it normally comes with the assumption that such a faith can be complete in itself without involving any practical action. The notion that people generally move from belief and then later to corresponding action is widely taken for granted within Western culture. While not saying that it doesn't happen at all, Western Christianity has not generally demonstrated a natural flow in moving from belief to practice. Instead, historians and social scientists have pointed out many discrepancies between belief and practice. As noted earlier, sometimes Christians have accommodated their beliefs to worldly practices. At other times they have segregated their beliefs from practical day-to-day living. The issue is not simply the universal problem of striving Christians falling short of their ideals. It is more than that—Western culture seems to stand out when it comes to a separation of belief from practice.

That an ideal can have a valid existence apart from concrete expression is rooted in ancient Greek philosophy. This form of thinking makes it easier for people to live with inconsistencies between their beliefs and their actions. One allows his or her belief in certain ideals to substitute for actual practice. Because so many people in Western society claim to hold Christian beliefs, it is assumed by many that Western society *lives* in a Christian manner. But this is not necessarily so.

An Epistle of Straw?

The Epistle of James speaks directly to the issue of belief detached from concrete action. James gets right to this problem of inconsistency found in so much of Western Christianity. Some Christians have discounted James and claim that it conflicts with the biblical teachings regarding grace. However, what James says about faith does not conflict with the teachings of Paul or the rest of the New Testament. Rather, James deals with correcting a distorted and false view of biblical faith. The general content of the Epistle of James focuses on Christian discipleship in practice. In particular, James attacks outright the "faith-as-belief-only" position.[8]

James targets the matter of belief separated from practice in chapter 2, verses 14–26. Here he argues passionately that true Christian faith is inseparable from works. Practical application must be involved as belief and practice form a unity. A Christian faith that is intellectual in nature and understood only in terms of belief is not truly faith. According to James, the "belief-only" faith:

has no soteriological value (2:14),

is completely dead (2:17),

has commonality with the demonic (2:19),

is useless and is foolish to hold on to (2:20),

is of a different nature than the faith of Abraham (2:21),

is incomplete (2:22) (probably the best that can be said for it), and

is comparable to a lifeless corpse (2:26).

Whereas within Western culture beliefs and ideals can have a kind of isolated existence in themselves, biblical faith cannot be divorced from practice. True Christian faith is organic, tangible, and demonstrated in action.

The question arises: was James aligning himself with the Christian Judaizers whom Paul attacked so much? James does not mention any of the Jewish ceremonial laws in his epistle. And when referring to the law, James identifies it as "the law of liberty" (James 1:25, 2:12), possibly alluding to the teachings of Paul and "the law of the Spirit" (see Romans 8:2). While James emphasizes many moral and ethical elements from the Old Testament, there are also numerous parallels with the Sermon on the Mount.

Of much importance is the fact that James confronts the root causes of social sin and secularization in his epistle. He speaks very directly to matters of prejudice, elitism, war, economic exploitation, hunger, practical spirituality, and cultural conformity. These are precisely the issues which so many Christians of "the South" fault Western Christianity for failing to address adequately. Problems with these specific issues may be linked to a flawed understanding of the Christian faith.

The problem James attacks—separating belief from practice—arises specifically out of a Greek-Hellenistic cultural context. Many biblical scholars agree that this particular section in James (verses 2:14–26) was not addressed primarily to Jewish Christians. While the epistle's Greek writing style implies a Greek-influenced audience, its content is very Hebraic. It has been suggested that James' argument concerning faith and works was directed specifically to those who had misinterpreted Paul's teaching about faith.[9] The point James is making can be applied to Greek-influenced Western culture over the centuries.

That Martin Luther did not see much worth in the Epistle of James is significant. He called it "an epistle of straw," barren in theological content.[10] Dietrich Bonhoeffer, the Lutheran theologian martyred under the Nazis, reflects on Luther and faith in his book, *The Cost of Discipleship*. According to Bonhoeffer, for the most part Luther lived a life of obedience and discipleship that was implied in his theology. But those who seized upon Luther's teachings did not take into account this implied life of obedience. The consequences have been what Bonhoeffer calls "cheap grace." It is a doctrine of grace without discipleship.[11] Nevertheless, it appears that Luther's attitude towards the Epistle of James and the room his teachings left for the development of "cheap grace" underscores an inherent weakness of Western Christianity when it comes to connecting belief to practice.

Separating Belief and Practice

It would be very difficult in the biblical Hebraic culture for the concept of faith unconnected to concrete life and practice to take root. Christian theologians outside of mainstream Western culture point this out and assert that only in Greek-rooted Western culture could theologians vehemently debate dogma while remaining indifferent to human slavery or the extermination of Jewish people. Distinctive qualities set apart Greek-Hellenistic thought from Hebraic thought. Hellenistic thought tends to be philosophical while Hebraic thought tends to be organic, concrete, and focused on real-life experience. For the Greeks, to "know" something was impersonal and intellectual. For the Hebrews, to "know" something was to encounter it personally. The Greek mind tried to make an image of reality analogous to a photograph; they searched for what today would be thought of as objective truth. The Hebrews had no such interest in a photographic view of reality. Greek thought tended to be abstract, and God, therefore, was to be found in the realm of "ideas." For the Israelites, God was revealed in history and human encounter. In the Greek context, Plato developed dichotomies and epistemological splits between the material and the spiritual, the secular and the sacred, the body and the soul. Such contemplation was alien to the Hebraic worldview.[12] It is this difference between Greek thought and Hebraic thought that sheds much light on why Western Christianity has had difficulty connecting belief to practice. We can understand how an unbiblical definition of faith-as-belief-alone could emerge from these Greek-Hellenistic roots.

It should be noted that the Hebraic context is very important for comprehending Scripture. In the early Church, the Gentiles were taught about God's actions in the history of the Jewish people as they were evangelized. The Old Testament was presented as if it were a part of their own past history. Christian faith was explained in relation to Abraham's faith. But allowing "faith" to take on the connotation of "belief only" results in a weak practice of Christian ethics and discipleship.[13]

Liberation theologians have identified Western Christianity's weakness of not speaking directly to real life situations, especially to those of the poor and the oppressed. James Cone points out that American whites in their theology are generally concerned with matters on a "spiritual" and "philosophical" level, while African-Americans are generally concerned with theology as it related to their struggle for liberation from racial oppression.[14] Latin American liberation theologians are also critical of the philosophical orientation of Western theology. Hugo Assman, Gustavo Gutierrez, and José Miguez Bonino are among the Latin American theologians who maintain that Christian truth and ideals cannot exist merely in the abstract without tangible historical expression. They assert that one can only speak of Christian truth within the context of real life situations.[15] While many of these theologians have tended to embrace Marxism and secular political action uncritically, their analysis of Western Christianity is very illuminating.

Ron Sider points to these same Greek-Hellenistic influences as one of the reasons why many Christians today do not embrace wholistic Christianity. He raises the issue of the sharp division some Christians have made between the "spiritual" and the "physical." Sider asks whether or not this originates from "Greek thought rather than from the Bible? Plato certainly considered the body evil and the soul good (and therefore more important). But did the Hebrew thinkers? Would Amos and Jesus understand and affirm the claim of Harold Lindsell that 'the mission of the church is preeminently spiritual [and] revolves around the non-material aspects of life.' In biblical thought is not the person a body-soul unity?"[16] Additionally, as many conservative churches focused on correct doctrine, they also tended to minimize practical application, especially with regard to social issues. Carl Ellis notes that their "dysfunctionality" resulted in part from how Western theology itself "had developed under the challenge of unbelieving philosophy and science, and thus it was much more concerned with *epistemological* issues (what we should know about God) than with *ethical* issues (how we should obey God)."[17] This dichotomization found in Western Christianity is not simply a result of cultural roots. However, the Western world's cultural milieu certainly contributes to this dichotomization. Recovering a wholistic Christianity requires an awareness of the limitations which come with these Greek-Hellenistic cultural influences.

Learning from African Theology

There is a significant non-Western approach to Christian theology taking place in Africa which can help us to reclaim an organic faith. In the past few decades, Christianity has grown rapidly in sub-Saharan Africa. Statistically, more than one-third of the people in that part of the continent claim church affiliation. Christianity continues to expand at such a rapid pace that some observers speculate that Africa will be the center of Christianity early in the twenty-first century. A vitality and richness is found in the faith and worship of great numbers of African Christians. While most Western missionaries brought to Africa a Christianity inseparable from Western culture, in recent decades a movement towards an indigenous African Christianity has taken place. African Christian leaders and theologians are now reconsidering traditional African culture. In the process they are discovering many parallels between traditional African culture and biblical Hebrew culture.

In traditional African culture, religious belief and practice are inseparable, pervading every aspect of life. Unlike Western culture, in the African context "there is no distinction between the sacred and the secular, between the religious and non-religious, between the spiritual and material areas of life."[18] The African theologian John Mbiti notes that African peoples are "notoriously religious." Formal written creeds are not necessary in traditional African religion because religion is lived. Mbiti notes that he has not come across a word for "religion" in his study of hundreds of traditional African languages. Religion is integrated with life and lived within the setting of community.

The aim of traditional African religion is not to philosophize or theologize about religion, but to live it. Here the "ideal" cannot be separated from the "real." In traditional African culture, abstract truth has little meaning or existence outside of life experiences.[19] Dr. Harold Turner, a leading scholar on the emerging African church, has observed that many African churches make greater use of James than of most other parts of the New Testament. The organic approach found in African traditional culture lends itself to a more wholistic understanding of Christian faith.[20]

Seeking Organic Faith

All Christians should embrace an organic faith incorporating practical action. This is a faith that works. It must be orthodox, evangelical, faithful to Scripture and to the gospel of Jesus Christ. Rather than being something new, organic faith gets back to the true biblical meaning of faith. Unfortunately, even the concept of orthodoxy has come to refer only to doctrine and not to practical action or lifestyle. Christian beliefs and practices should form an inseparable unity. A geometric analogy may be helpful in grasping the meaning of an organic faith. A person only able to see things in two dimensions would never understand the meaning of three-dimensional reality. Organic faith can be compared to a three-dimensional object. Beliefs on an intellectual level would be two-dimensional. While these dimensions are an indispensable part of faith, alone they are incomplete and distorted. When the third dimension—i.e. practical action—is included, only then does one have a complete realization of faith.[21]

While concrete action should be essential, the intellectual, philosophical, and doctrinal aspects must not in any way be dropped as necessary components of Christian faith. Such an organic faith should not be confused with existentialist theology and its "escape from reason," with the mind completely left behind. The gospel needs to be communicated to the Western mind with the same cultural sensitivity that is required in other places. Yet even here, the presentation of Christian truth needs to draw much more on historical, sociological, and experiential reality.

In the call of Christians to an organic faith, the question remains of whether or not such a faith is merely a movement toward legalism. In Galatians 1:6 Paul calls this legalism "another gospel." Does Paul oppose concrete Christian practice or consider it to be in a realm of secondary importance? A Western mind might read this into Paul's writings. Paul is only against concrete practices—works—coming from a system other than the person of Jesus Christ. In Phillipians 3:9 Paul talks about his own emancipation from Jewish legalism. He says, "I am not dependent upon any of the self-achieved righteousness of the Law. God has given me that genuine righteousness which comes from faith in Christ" (PHILLIPS). In Ephesians 2:10 Paul says that Christians are "created in Christ Jesus to do good works" (NIV). It is only by God's grace and mercy that we can live a distinct life of obedience that otherwise would be impossible.

Paul strongly argues against the misuse of the doctrine of grace (see Romans 6:15–23). The death and resurrection of

Christ are both an atonement for our sins *and* the means by which we are brought into a new life of obedience.[22] For Paul as well as James, belief and obedient action form an inseparable unity. He refers continually to a faith connected to practical living.[23] In Romans 1:5 he says that the very purpose of the gospel is to bring people into "the obedience of faith" (NRSV). In Romans 6:18, Paul bolsters the point by declaring, "You have been set free from sin and have become slaves to righteousness" (NIV). The expression "obedience of faith" is used repeatedly in Paul's letter to the Romans and gives support to the position that obedience is a quality of faith itself. As Bonhoeffer tells us, only the person who believes is obedient, and only the person who is obedient believes.[24]

Action Rooted in Christ

True biblical faith is not only organic, it is rooted in Jesus Christ—the author and finisher of our faith (Hebrews 12:2). Works connected to this faith are distinguished in that they begin and end in Christ. There are three basic qualities separating Christian practice from the world's. The first is *motivation*. Christian practice springs forth from Christian commitment and discipleship. The second quality involves *power*. In Christ there is power to live out Christian practice. With so many spiritual, social, and psychological forces working to lead people into worldly conformity, the Holy Spirit gives us power to live in obedience to Christ. Lastly, the actual *content* or style of Christian practice is unique. Christians are not limited to mimicking the behavior patterns and actions of others. Although much can be learned from the actions of non-Christians, the Christian presence in the world should produce distinctive actions. The witness, and even the apologetic, of the Church should be something observable.[25] God produces a tangible reality in the world impossible for humanity to produce by itself. The orthodoxy of organic faith is summed up in the words of Jesus, "Apart from me you can do nothing" (John 15:5b NIV).

We need a complete acknowledgment of Western culture's distorting effect on the meaning of Christian faith. A "faith-as-belief-only" definition of the Christian faith should be rejected as passionately as it is in the Epistle of James. True orthodoxy takes hold of a faith that brings belief and practice into a unity. To the evangelical formula of the Reformation—only Christ, only Scripture—is to be included: only *organic* faith, a faith that works.

6

I WASN'T LISTENING TO THE SERMON (ON THE MOUNT)

The Book of James may direct us away from a faith without works, but it can also point us toward the Sermon on the Mount found in the Gospel of Matthew, chapters five through seven. This is the place Christians need to look in order to reclaim a faith that makes a difference in the way they live.

A number of years ago, I attended a small group Bible study on the Sermon on the Mount. I was startled as the leader of the study advocated the position that the Sermon on the Mount was simply a gospel of works, not to be confused with the gospel of grace. Although he acknowledged that these were the very words of Jesus, he dismissed their relevance by using dispensationalist reasoning. For him, the Sermon on the

Mount was only for the age to come and not for the current "age of grace." He claimed that the Sermon was like the Law in the Old Testament; although helpful, it was a distraction for Christians to take it literally at this point in time. While presenting this view, he strongly maintained that his theology was conservative and faithful to Scripture. In fact, what he was doing was making central teachings of Christ irrelevant in the same way liberal theologians are often accused of doing.

The Kingdom Revolution

This Bible study leader is not alone. Many who claim a literal and conservative view of Scripture show a reluctance to apply this same view for the Sermon on the Mount. If they did, not only would it challenge some of their beliefs, it would also challenge many aspects of their lifestyle in society.

The Sermon on the Mount can be regarded as a summary of the teachings of Christ. It is about God's kingdom, called the "kingdom of heaven" in Matthew's Gospel. Christians should have at the center of their thought and practice an understanding of the "kingdom of God."[1] In *The Community of the King*, Howard A. Snyder calls attention to the failure of the modern church to uphold the biblical perspective of God's Kingdom. He tells us that "neither evangelism nor social action make full sense divorced from the fact of the Christian community as the visible, earthly expression of the Kingdom of God."[2] Talking about the "kingdom of God" may confuse some, as this phrase is often associated with the Jehovah's Witnesses. Yet many of us who consider ourselves biblical

Christians are deficient in grasping fully what the kingdom of God is and how it relates to our life in society today.

There is a sharp contrast between the kingdom of God and the kingdoms of the world. Jesus tells Pilate, "My kingdom is not of this world" (John 18:36 NIV). He explains that his kingdom is unlike any Pilate has ever encountered. Jesus illustrates this as he tells Pilate, "If my kingdom belonged to this world, my followers would fight to keep me from being handed over to the Jewish authorities" (John 18:36 TEV). The kingdom of God is a distinct departure from worldliness, or world-centered actions.

The world and the kingdom are controlled by different realities. In its natural state, the world is controlled by what Scripture calls "principalities and powers" (Ephesians 6:12 KJV). These principalities and powers are ultimately controlled by Satan, the Evil One.[3] In Matthew 4, the chapter preceding the Sermon on the Mount, one sees how the principalities and powers of the world operate. As noted earlier, the things Satan offers Christ—physical resources, social recognition, and the power of the state—together have overwhelming control over people's lives. These forces constantly pull at Christians to draw them into worldly conformity rather than into kingdom living.[4]

The Poor In Spirit

Within the Sermon on the Mount can be found the Beatitudes (Matthew 5:3–11), which are considered to be a summary of the Sermon itself. The first beatitude is a cornerstone for the entire Sermon: "Blessed are the poor in spirit for theirs is the kingdom of heaven" (NIV). Some modern translations, in an attempt to adopt more contemporary English, use the word "happy" in place of "blessed." In modern culture, the word "happy" generally refers to a superficial, fleeting mood. "Blessed" implies a deeper happiness. The Today's English Version (TEV) or Good News Bible (which provides an excellent translation of the Sermon of the Mount) labels the Beatitudes "True Happiness," and this is what is meant here.

"Those who know they are spiritually poor" (TEV) are positioned to receive the blessings of the kingdom of God. It isn't enough simply to be spiritually poor; it is the *realization* of this state that counts. All people are under God's judgment; yet, while spiritual poverty engulfs everyone, many do not recognize it. The story of the Pharisee and the tax collector in Luke 18:10–14 illustrates this beatitude. Jesus tells us about two people who went to the Temple to pray. "'The Pharisee stood apart by himself and prayed, 'I thank you, God that I am not greedy, dishonest, or an adulterer, like everybody else. I thank you that I am not like that tax collector over there. I fast two days a week and I give you one tenth of all my income.' But the tax collector stood at a distance and would not even raise his face to heaven, but beat on his breast and said, 'God, have mercy on me, a sinner!'" (TEV). Jesus tells us that the tax collector went home with something; the Pharisee did not. "The poor in spirit are not the proud in spirit," states Clarence Jordan in his book, *The Sermon on the Mount.*[5]

Some think that after their conversion they no longer have to be "poor in spirit." This thinking is misguided. Recognizing our spiritual need is an ongoing quality of the genuine

Christian life. Much can be said for Eastern Orthodox Christianity, which emphasizes the quality of spiritual humility. In this tradition, there is a recognition that spiritual growth comes as one realizes more and more the need for God's forgiveness and mercy. We see this in the warning given to the church of Laodicea in Revelation: "You say, 'I am rich; I have acquired wealth and do not need a thing.' But you do not realize that you are wretched, pitiful, poor, blind, and naked." (Revelation 3:17 NIV). Churches should see themselves as spiritually poor before God. As a person grows in Christ, he or she should be praying passionately more and more like the tax collector, "God, have mercy on me, a sinner!"

This first beatitude is the *sine qua non* of God's kingdom. But should spiritual poverty be acknowledged only with respect to personal sins? What about social sins whereby people participate on a collective level? When Isaiah has a vision in which he finds himself before the throne of God, he says these words: "Woe to me! . . . I am ruined! For I am a man of unclean lips, and I live among a people of unclean lips, and my eyes have seen the King, the Lord Almighty." (Isaiah 6:5 NIV). He does not separate himself from the social sin of his people. Isaiah did not need a degree in sociology to see that he too was caught up in social sin. God used Isaiah to call Israel's attention to the social sin that the Israelites took for granted. The modern split between societal sin and personal sin is absent. Spiritual poverty before God involves an awareness of both.[6]

Christians involved in social action should not set themselves apart by praying, "Thank you, God, that I am not a racist, an exploiter, a sexist, a plunderer of the environment, etc." Sadly, the impression given by many Christian activists is not one of spiritual humility. They often have a pharisaical attitude towards "them." Such attitudes of self-righteousness can appear in situations involving either social or personal sin.

As Jesus goes on to address particular moral laws in the Sermon on the Mount, he instructs that pharisaical attitudes must give way to spiritual poverty. For example, the issue is not whether one has actually committed the act of adultery; if someone has only looked at another with lust, then adultery has already been committed in that person's heart (see Matthew 5:28). Likewise, some white people point fingers self-righteously at other white people guilty of blatant racial prejudice while at the same time denying any prejudice whatsoever in themselves. In many cases these same people want to tell African-Americans how best to fight racial prejudice. The closer one draws to Christ, the more such arrogance gives way to an admission of one's own complicity in social sin.

Those Who Mourn

There is an order to the Beatitudes. They are not random sayings, but are like steps into the kingdom.[7] The mourning Jesus speaks of in the second beatitude follows spiritual humility; "Happy are those who mourn; God will comfort them!" (TEV). This beatitude can be understood in two ways. What immediately comes to mind is normal human sadness. For example, we may think of someone grieving over the loss of a loved one. Scripture affirms that when people go through the grieving process, drawing close to God gives them strength to endure. However, the Bible talks about mourning for more than personal loss and disappointments.

Jesus weeps over Jerusalem. In the Old Testament, the prophets weep over the reality that their nation has ignored God and followed the practices of other nations. Those who practice kingdom values should be deeply concerned about the tragedies of the world around them. We should grieve over our society's captivity to sin. Christians should experience inner pain when seeing humankind, so capable of greatness, prone to self-destruction.[8] We are to mourn over injustice and the pain people suffer as a result. Mourning is a response to the state of our world and our own complicity in it. In the Book of James, we read, "Come near to God and he will come near to you. Wash your hands, you sinners, and purify your hearts, you double-minded. Grieve, mourn and wail. Change your laughter to mourning and your joy to gloom. Humble yourselves before the Lord, and he will lift you up" (James 4:8-10 NIV). God doesn't abandon people who mourn in this way; they receive comfort. And they are not paralyzed by guilt.

The Meek

"Blessed are the meek, for they will inherit the earth" (NIV) is the third beatitude. There is some confusion over what is meant by *meek* here. Does this mean that people should allow others to "run all over" them? Is meekness really *weakness*? The question is particularly pressing in relationship to the oppressed. Many associate meekness with what African-Americans call an

"Uncle Tom" attitude. While those in power may use such interpretations to keep the oppressed in line, the Bible refers to another type of meekness. It is not meekness in the face of an exploitive oppressor, but submissiveness towards God. Scripture calls Moses and Jesus meek in this respect. Neither Moses' dealing with Pharaoh nor Jesus' overturning of the currency and exchange market in the Temple can be described as passively meek. They are neither intimidated nor fearful in their actions. Rather, dealing with people who are meek before God is dealing, in effect, with God Himself. God will win— and such people *will* "inherit the earth." Another way of translating this beatitude is, "Blessed are those whose wills are submitted to God's will because *they cannot be stopped.*"[10]

Such an understanding of meekness leading to victory can be found in the African-American spirituals developed during slavery. Slaves would sing about Jesus, "the Captain who never lost a battle." When people have their wills submitted to God's will, they become fearless and act with courage even when the odds are against them. Such a meekness should be a distinguishing feature of Christians as they involve themselves in social concern and the struggle against injustice. This involves a daily seeking of God's guidance for practical action. It should also be recognized that there are many different approaches to confronting social issues. What may seem a "solution" to one issue may lead to a whole new set of problems. Social activists have a tendency to get so caught up in their causes that they develop blind spots. Praying for direction and taking a stance of meekness before God is critical to making a lasting difference.

Hungering for God's Will

The first three beatitudes speak of relinquishing pride, self-righteousness, and complacency. The next four talk of qualities Christians should adopt as citizens of God's kingdom. "Happy are those whose greatest desire is to do what God requires; God will satisfy them fully!" (TEV). This is also translated as "Blessed are those who hunger and thirst for righteousness, for they will be filled" (NIV). This beatitude is critical for describing the way Christians are to approach the question of ethics.

During the time of Christ, the Jewish people did not struggle with the issue of ethics as people do in the modern world. Many people today view ethics as relativistic. The Jewish people generally accepted the Law of Moses. But the Bible shows that the Law in itself does not have the power to change what goes on deep down inside people's hearts. Indeed, we find widespread inconsistency, hypocrisy, and self-deception similar to what the Apostle Paul admits to in Romans chapter 7. Paul says that the commandment, the Law, brought him death. It was not because the commandment was wrong. He says, "It was sin that killed me by using something good." Paul goes on to explain by saying, "We know that the Law is spiritual. But I am merely a human, and I have been sold as a slave to sin" (Romans 7:13 b, 14 CEV). Further along in the sermon, Jesus addresses this problem of how something good—the Law—can be twisted into something sinful. Jesus describes how we can break some of the Ten Commandments in our hearts while maintaining that we are keeping them. This is done by focusing only on external behavior (Matthew 5:21–30). In addition, people come up with loopholes, attempting to justify actions contrary to the spirit of the Law (see Matthew 5:31–37). Also, some carry out "religious" acts for show or out of other impure motives (see Matthew 6:1–8).[10] And so we find people who seem to be doing right, really doing wrong.

The kind of righteousness called for in God's kingdom is one from the heart. One hungers and thirsts for this sort of righteousness. Prophecies concerning the Messiah announced that the Law would be written on people's hearts (Jeremiah 31:33). It is not a righteousness defined by what the majority of people consider right. Instead, it is "doing what God requires." God sets the standard for both personal and social righteousness. This righteousness encompasses one's relationship to God, to neighbor, to oneself, and even towards the environment. It is wholistic.

Again, some people play down this beatitude because it seems to draw people into legalism. Yet, almost any of the moral teachings of Jesus can be taken out of context and used legalistically. On the other hand, if a person is not "hungering and thirsting after righteousness," then what is he or she seeking after for fulfillment? In Jeremiah 9:23–24, we read, " 'Let not the wise man boast in his wisdom or the strong man boast of his strength or the rich man boast of his riches, but let him who boasts boast about this: that he understands and knows me, that I am the Lord, who exercises kindness, justice and righteousness on earth, for in these I delight,' declares the Lord" (NIV). Nations get caught up in the pursuit of brain power, technology, prosperity, and military might in place of

God's righteousness. One ultimately finds fulfillment only when he or she hungers and thirsts to see God's righteousness practiced upon the earth.

The Merciful

"Happy are those who are merciful to others; God will be merciful to them!" (TEV). Mercy here is referring to compassion for people in need. The Greek word found in the original text is distinguished from the Greek word referring to grace. This kind of mercy is illustrated in the story of the good Samaritan who "showed mercy." The world lacks this kind of mercy. Concern for people in need—the destitute, the homeless, the poor—is not a priority for much of the world. Yet such mercy and compassion are high on the agenda of citizens of the kingdom.[11] Christians are to follow the example of Christ in ministering to the physical, emotional, and spiritual needs of people. God's love, shown to us in Jesus Christ, must be reflected in our actions towards others. Some people come up with rationalizations to avoid showing mercy in this way. They may find a way to blame victims for their own plight. Some go on to claim that by giving help, "these people" are prevented from helping themselves.

Seeing God

"Happy are the pure in heart; they will see God!" (TEV) is the sixth beatitude. This is a high step in the progression of the Beatitudes as it deals with the heart, the center of a person's being. Now the issue of inner motives comes into full view.

The pure in heart are those who do not have divided loyalties or mixed motives. For example, they do not bring attention to themselves when they are helping the needy (Matthew 6:2).

When someone experiences a second birth in Christ, the old nature begins to give way to a new nature. The new nature is God's own nature implanted inside. Paul speaks of this in Romans: "You do not live as your human nature tells you to; instead, you live as the Spirit tells you to—if, in fact, God's Spirit lives in you" (Romans 8:9 TEV). When a person is in Christ, he or she breaks with the old life and its idolatries of money, power, social prestige, and self-seeking pleasure. Yet these old idols seem to find all kinds of subtle ways to remain in the life of Christians. This happens because the surrounding culture has institutionalized many of these idolatries. Clarence Jordan says that when people try to keep their eyes on two different masters (i.e., idols), they find that they become cross-eyed (Matthew 6:22–24).[12] The wooden and stone idols mentioned in the Old Testament are not at all referred to in the Sermon on the Mount. Instead, the idols of self, status, and money are highlighted. These idols of the heart are cleansed only as Christ works within our human nature.

The Peacemakers

"Happy are those who work for peace; God will call them his children!" (TEV). The Bible describes God as peacemaker. The Messiah is described as the "Prince of Peace" (Isaiah 9:6 b). Therefore, peacemaking is a divine work and it naturally follows that peacemakers, bearing God's image, will be called his children.

Peace is sometimes confused with an absence of conflict. In many parts of the world, shots are not actually being fired between two parties, yet few would claim that the people are coexisting in a state of peace. Peace is a deeper reality. What is helpful here is the Hebrew word *shalom*. *Shalom* means more than a cessation of conflict. As Eldin Villafañe tells us, "Shalom speaks of wholeness, soundness, completeness, health, harmony, reconciliation, justice, welfare—both personal and social."[13] It is a complete peace involving peace with God, with neighbor, with self, and even with creation. This peacemaking encompasses evangelism, the work of reconciling people in conflict, and helping individuals receive peace of mind. Such comprehensive peacemaking must be the vision and commitment of all who want to follow Christ.

The Reaction of the World

When the kingdom of God is lived out in the world, there is a reaction. Many people have heard the expression, "When God acts, Satan reacts." The kingdom of God breaks into the world and challenges it with something the world cannot harness. It threatens those whose loyalty is first and foremost to the things of the world. Various forms of persecution are bound to come to those who follow Jesus Christ. This does not mean that Christians should go about looking for negative reactions by aggravating others. Christians should work against any tendency towards an unhealthy martyr complex. On the other hand, there are undoubtedly some adverse consequences for living the kingdom lifestyle in the world. Yet even in this, there is a blessing. The blessing is the identification with Jesus. "If the world hates you, keep in mind that it hated me first," Jesus tells his disciples (John 15:18 NIV). People of the world look first for the praise and the rewards of the world. Those of God's kingdom look for heavenly rewards.

Up until now the Beatitudes have begun with "Happy are those." Now Jesus begins addressing his disciples in the second person. He says to them, "Happy are you when people insult you and persecute you and tell all kinds of evil lies against you because you are my followers. Be happy and glad, for a great reward is kept for you in heaven. This is how the prophets who lived before you were persecuted" (Matthew 5:11-12 TEV). We know that both Christians and non-Christians receive persecution for doing right in the world. However, Christians are subjected to further persecution even by allies involved in social concern. They are persecuted for their identification with Jesus. Jesus is not just another teacher or religious leader, he is the king of the kingdom. The Sermon is now put into perspective. One cannot be part of the kingdom without accepting Jesus Christ. He is the Messiah, the one talked about in the Book of Daniel who was to come and establish a kingdom that has no end.

The Salt of the Earth

"You are like salt for all mankind. But if salt loses its saltiness, there is no way to make it salty again. It has become worthless, so it is thrown out and people trample on it" (Matthew 5:13

TEV). These words follow the Beatitudes. The Beatitudes talk of humility, mourning, meekness, and a happiness found even in the midst of persecution. This opposes the messages given by the world. The world fosters the love of pride, power, and popularity. The Sermon challenges these worldly values. It calls for a spiritual revolution, a radical change within. Here, a new value system is advocated. Without the things the world says are needed for success, this kingdom movement might appear to have little chance of making a difference. Yet the Sermon proclaims the opposite. Those willing to give up their inner hold on the things of the world are best positioned to make a drastic, revolutionary impact on the world. Because this so completely contradicts conventional thinking, one must ask, how can this be?

Standing in sharp contrast to the world, the kingdom of God offers no safe haven for evil. It doesn't tolerate the world's mess as a natural condition to which people can only resign themselves. Yet followers of Christ really have the world at heart. Comparing God's people to salt is to say that we are to play a redemptive role in our society and our world.

Salt functions in different ways and has many uses. First, it is a seasoning for food. Vibrant Christians bring a special flavoring to the world. This flavoring transforms the cultures of the world. Paul tells the believers in Corinth, "We Christians have the unmistakable 'scent' of Christ, discernible alike to those who are being saved and to those who are heading for death" (2 Corinthians 2:15 PHILLIPS). Salt is also a preservative. In places where there is little or no refrigeration, salt is used to preserve meat and fish and other food items. Salt has a purifying, disinfectant quality. The influence of the followers of Jesus has a restraining effect on a world heading towards death and destruction. War, the havoc caused by racism and ethnic friction, the casual attitude towards abortion, the destruction of the environment, the disintegration of family, and the decline of moral values are all moving the world towards decay. When Christians function as salt, they help to make the world more "kosher."

Why aren't many churches having an impact on their surrounding society? The reason is that their conformity to the social environment takes the "salt" out of their witness. Such churches no longer function as a preservative. Jacques Ellul provides insights regarding this preservation quality in his book, *The Presence of the Kingdom*. He tells us that "the will of the world is always a will to death, a will to suicide." He goes on to say that Christians "must not accept this suicide, and we must so act that it cannot take place. So we must know what is the actual form of the world's will to suicide in order that we may oppose it, in order that we may know how, and in what direction, we ought to direct our efforts."[14]

The events in the West African nation of Liberia between the late 1970s and early 1990s provided me with an opportunity to see a society march towards self-destruction. Liberia was settled by repatriated African-Americans in the early 1800s, with the model having already been set by its neighbor, Sierra Leone. Those who resettled, and their descendants known as Americo-Liberians, established a government paralleling that of the United States. Over the years Americo-Liberians maintained a tight control over the country even though the indigenous ethnic groups were actually in the majority. The Americo-Liberians oppressed and discriminated against people from the indigenous ethnic groups. However, more than anywhere else in Africa, American influence was greatest in Liberia, especially in the capital city of Monrovia named after the American President James Monroe. On the surface it seemed that there was also a dominant Christian influence. Liberia in 1977 seemed to me to be overevangelized as I saw numerous American-sponsored missionary groups and churches saturating the entire country. The president was a Baptist minister, the vice president was a Methodist bishop, churches were filled, and every other taxicab appeared to be tuned in to the local Christian radio station. At the same time, Liberia had major unresolved tensions below the surface.

The American-sponsored missionary groups seemed comfortable with all of the transplanted American culture and were not very critical of the injustices faced by the indigenous ethnic groups. A major upheaval took place in 1980 when the president was assassinated and the government was overthrown. The assassin, Samuel Doe, was hailed as a hero by many of the indigenous groups and pronounced president. Unfortunately, it did not take long for this new government to become more repressive than the one it replaced. Later, barbaric civil war erupted during which tens of thousands of innocent civilians were brutally murdered. The country disintegrated into chaos. Before 1980, many Liberian Christians allowed the oppression of the indigenous people by American-influenced Americo-Liberians to go unchallenged. Following 1980, Christians from the indigenous groups also suspended critical judgment as they cheered an assassin. When the civil war started in the early 1990s, a demonic frenzy was suddenly let loose. Yet the seeds of destruction were there all along. For all the seeming influence of Christians, their record was very poor when it came to challenging injustice, cultural imperialism, violence, and power madness. The church had allowed itself to be comfortable in worldly conformity. Jesus gives a warning to Christians when they are not serving as salt. When salt becomes just like the rest of the food without making a real difference, it certainly does become worthless.[15]

The term "the salt of the earth" is also referenced in Leviticus 2:13: "Put salt on every grain offering, because salt represents the covenant between you and God" (TEV). The world should not only see good works, but also the covenantal relationship with God to which the good works point. Not only should Christians work to keep the world from destruction, but they should also serve as a light to the world.

Impact on the World

"You are like light for the whole world. A city built on a hill cannot be hid" (Matthew 5:19 TEV). C. S. Lewis once said that he believed in Christianity as he believed in the sun, not only because he saw it, but also because by the sun he was able to see everything else. Not only should Christians "see through" the world and its movement towards death, they should also be able to show the world the way to life. Light in this sense does not only refer to intellectual head knowledge. Nor is it merely a kind of esoteric enlightenment which one finds in Hinduism and other Eastern religions. What is implied is that Christians ought to live as a city built on a hill that cannot be hid. This means a visible demonstration of light reflected through our actions in the real world.

"Your light must shine before people, so that they will see the good things you do and praise your Father in heaven" (Matthew 5:16 TEV). Christians ought not to blend into conformity, but should live and act as light in their communities. These "good things" done by followers of Christ should turn people's praise not to Christians, but to God. The reference here is to living acts performed in the world, not far off in some isolated community or behind the closed doors of a church building. The end result is that people praise God in heaven because Christians are bringing something heavenly to earth. The source of these "good things" is Jesus Christ, the light of the world, the One who has come down from heaven. This is the difference that the Christian presence makes in the world. A new lifestyle is lived out in the world, yet its origin is not of the world. This is the transformity noted in Romans 12:2.

The Sermon on the Mount is the Christian manifesto, outlining the kingdom of God as the source of a radical transformation in the real world. Far too many of us Christians have slept right through this sermon, yet few other sermons will make any sense until we really begin to pay attention to this one.

7

A DISTINCT COMMUNITY

There is no better way of affirming the Sermon on the Mount than for Christians to live together in love. God calls Christians into community. It is not an optional feature, but a core ingredient of living the lifestyle of faith. This fellowship—known as *koinonia* in New Testament Greek—is a here and now demonstration of God's healing of humanity's brokenness and alienation. When Christians allow God's Spirit to make the church into a community of love, the entanglement of hatred and fear begins to unravel. Francis Schaeffer calls attention to John 17:21 and claims that this unity in love among Christians is "the final apologetic" before the world.[1] Yet forming community which breaks down entrenched barriers comes only through God's grace amid struggle and difficulty.

The problem is that many want cheap community or a superficial unity. In December of 1970, I attended my first

InterVarsity Urbana Missionary Convention while serving as the chairperson of the New York area student committee. Months before the convention, a number of us students from New York City committed ourselves to making a difference at the upcoming gathering. We did not believe that such issues as racial prejudice and poverty would be recognized. Already, New York IVCF students had organized pre-Urbana workshops with topics such as "World Missions and Neo-Colonialism." It would not be business as usual at Urbana '70.

Months before the convention, with the encouragement of IVCF president Dr. John Alexander and others in national leadership, young black evangelical leaders such as Elward Ellis, Paul Gibson, Ron Potter, and Carl Ellis labored to recruit African-American students to attend Urbana '70. With greater awareness of racial prejudice from the civil rights movement, some of the leaders of InterVarsity started to examine their own organization. They began to think about the fact that African-Americans were not fully represented either in the InterVarsity movement or at the Urbana conventions. From the perspective of African-American Christian students, InterVarsity was a "white" organization, irrelevant to their experience. At this time, only one black staff worker served with InterVarsity's campus ministry in the entire United States. InterVarsity chapters did not exist at any of the historically black colleges. Furthermore, there was racial prejudice at work within local chapters. Widespread reports circulated of African-Americans being shunned when they showed up at local chapter meetings. Many African-American students felt their reception at the

Urbana '70 gathering would not be any different. The story was circulated that at the 1967 Urbana Convention, a major commotion erupted over a claim by one of the main speakers. The speaker, who was white, talked about the importance of Christians seeking to marry other believers. There was a major stir when he said he would rather marry a black committed Christian woman than someone of his own race who was not a committed Christian.

In 1970, the New York City InterVarsity chapters were very different in their ethnic and racial makeup from those found elsewhere in the United States. The city had a high percentage of students native to New York who commuted to college. Surveys also showed that more than ninety percent of all Protestants in New York City at this time were either African-American or belonged to other minority ethnic groups. The two staff workers in the city, Conrad Sauer and Paul Gibson, brought much sensitivity to the local context and its ethnic diversity. The IVCF chapters were growing rapidly in numbers as they incorporated students of diverse backgrounds. Barbara Benjamin, a volunteer staff worker, would later write *The Impossible Community,* which told of the development of this diversity at the IVCF chapter at Brooklyn College.[2] But many New York City students did not have positive experiences when they ventured beyond these local InterVarsity activities. They encountered racial prejudice at regional InterVarsity gatherings where it was reported that African-American students were simply being ignored.

African-American students in 1970 were feeling the impact

of the black power movement which followed on the heels of the earlier civil rights movement. At that time, African-American Christians had to encounter taunts from other African-American students about their association with the "white man's religion." To be in tune with the times, one had to reject Christianity and even the black church. Young black students felt compelled to consider Islam or some type of radical, even violent, political course of action. In a sociology course I was taking at the time, one of the students gave a class presentation explaining systematic oppression. The following week this student lost his limbs in an explosion that killed another person. Unknown to most of his peers, he had been involved in a black radical cell group engaged in bomb making.

Because Christianity was seen as part of the race problem, African-American Christian students felt they had extra burdens to bear. First, they were rejected by other black students for being Christian. Then, they experienced rejection by white Christian students for being black. Yet, rather than despair, many felt a sense of mission in going to Urbana '70.

When students arrived at the Urbana Convention, they discovered that a computer program had scattered them to different dorm assignments. The intention was for students from various places and backgrounds to have opportunities for interchange. But those from New York City had a need to stay together. Soul Liberation, an African-American contemporary music group, was invited to perform at Urbana '70. The group traveled to Urbana in chartered buses along with students from the New York area. Two full buses were identified as reserved for Soul Liberation. The extra seating was assigned to InterVarsity chapters with large numbers of black students. This group would be exempt from the computer scattering. Tom Skinner, a well-known black evangelist from New York City, had already been invited as one of the plenary speakers. The stage was being set. We felt that not only would God use the convention to speak to us, but God would also use us in some way to speak to the convention.

During the first full day of the convention, free time was scheduled in the afternoon. Students were encouraged to view displays by the various mission agencies in the Huff Gym. Here, while I walked with two other students from New York City, Panzy and Pauline Mullings, the idea came up to initiate a black caucus. In the official program there was a panel discussion on black Americans in foreign mission. This panel, moderated by Bill Pannell, was scheduled for later in the afternoon. We decided to circulate around the gym and tell the black students to gather an hour before this panel meeting. About seventy-five people came together as a result of word-of-mouth invitations. I then found myself standing in front of the group having to lead matters from there.

As I began to lead a discussion on our common concerns as African-American Christian students, someone raised the issue of whites being present. Others also spoke up to say that they were invited to a caucus in which African-Americans would have the opportunity to talk among themselves. In the auditorium there were a number of whites present, including a reporter from a leading news magazine. A heated dispute erupted over the issue of excluding nonblacks. It became very difficult for me to maintain order in the discussion. When Bill Pannell showed up to moderate his panel, I was greatly relieved. After his session finished, the caucus remained to continue its discussion. An agreement was made that those present should spread the word to other black students that the caucus was to continue after the evening plenary session. It would be held in a large meeting room in the same building where Soul Liberation and other New York City students were residing.

Tom Skinner was contacted and asked to moderate the caucus that evening. The interest in this forum was underscored as the room filled up with a large number of black students. But again, a significant number of white students came and took seats. The first issue addressed was whether or not to include them in the discussion. After much debate—painful and emotional at times—we voted to ask them to leave. A provision was made to have an open meeting scheduled for the last night the caucus would meet. Many of those who left claimed that the caucus was a black separatist group, practicing reverse discrimination. They formed their own group to pray for us. In the caucus sessions, African-American students shared their experiences of prejudice by white Christians and the conflicts it caused. People noted that merely singing "We are one in the Spirit" and talking about Christian love did not mean the end to racial discrimination among Christians. We struggled intensely over how to respond as Christians to the racial prejudice we were experiencing. Much time was given for prayer although the sessions went very late into the evening. Three overall commitments came out of the sessions. First, there was a commitment to outreach and evangelism directed at African-American students. Second, there was a commitment to working for black and white racial reconciliation. Last, people made a commitment to set up a national network of black Christian students. (Years later, the national IVCF organization incorporated a special component aimed at similar objectives.)

At the last caucus meeting, held with white students present, it became clear that the time spent alone had been necessary. In the joint meeting, African-Americans students had to address a large number of white students expressing their own prejudicial attitudes without any awareness that they had a problem. One Caucasian, who said he was a policeman, stood up to say that he wasn't partial to anyone. He noted that he had recently given a white person a driving ticket. He went on to say that at another time he had shot a black man for stealing. The feeling among the African-American students was that they would not have had any time to help each other if they had been compelled to spend all the caucus sessions responding to the issues raised by the whites. Many felt that only through the separate sessions was there a real chance for reconciliation. If we had glossed over deep issues, only a cheap unity would have resulted.[3]

At a plenary session, Tom Skinner gave what is considered the most memorable address of the convention: "The Liberator Has Come." Black students arrived early on the evening of his talk, sitting directly in front of the podium to give him support in the traditional black church style. One could sense the discomfort among the audience of more than 13,000 assembled in the arena, especially as he talked about racial oppression and the support that many Christians gave to it. When he ended his message by referring to Jesus Christ as the only true revolutionary, he received a rousing standing ovation.

As a result of the 1970 Urbana, InterVarsity began a process of change as African-American and other minority staff were recruited. Years later, IVCF developed Black Campus Ministries to focus its work with African-Americans students. This was later followed by a wider ethnic ministries division. Future Urbana conventions included official meeting times for black students. At Urbana '79 and Urbana '90, I did not find any whites present at these special meetings. Nor did I hear of any white students complaining of exclusion. By striving to recognize real issues of racial prejudice and unequal representation superficial unity was rejected by that first caucus. The group was working toward genuine community.

The New Community

The 1970 Urbana brought home to many the need for a biblical perspective on Christian community; one that did not simply gloss over deep and complicated divisions. God created humanity for community. People were created to live in peace and harmony. Sin disrupted and distorted the togetherness and community for which God created us. Over time, tensions and hatreds have developed within and between nations. The world watched numerous ethnic conflicts erupt with the breakup of the Soviet Union. Many ethnic groups and sub-groups through-out the world refuse to recognize certain outsiders as equals. They use cultural differences to foster hate, and this malice incites hostility and violence. More subtly, this causes mental stress and anguish because bad feelings towards others sap a person's energy. Psychoanalyst Erich Fromm pointed out in his writings that one's mental health is dependent on one's ability to love and be loved by others. Although human beings have a need for community, we also have a tendency towards discrimi-nation, exploitation, and vengeance. Instead of shining as a light, many churches simply reflect the disunity surrounding them. How can Christians move towards real community, one reflecting agape, God's love?

In 1 Corinthians, Paul presents the Corinthians with God's plan for living in community. He gets right to the point: "I beg you in the name of the Lord Jesus Christ to stop arguing among yourselves. Let there be real harmony so that there won't be splits in the church. I plead with you to be of one mind, united in thought and purpose" (1 Corinthians 1:10 TLB). Holding wrong beliefs was not their problem. Nor were they lacking with regard to spiritual gifts and talents. Here was a church made up of believers in Christ, but each convert had brought old prejudices of class, gender, and race into their church relationships. Paul reminds them that when Christ comes into a person's life, the person begins a new way of living out social relationships. In his second letter to the Corinthian church, he writes, "So if anyone is in Christ, there is a new creation; everything old has passed away; see, everything has become new" (2 Corinthians 5:17 NRSV). They were not living as a new community in Christ.

By God's Grace

Three biblical principles emerge as the basis of true Christian community. The first is a centering on Christ as the one creating and instituting community. This means accepting our own powerlessness to produce real community. Rather than relying on ourselves, we are to rely upon the work of the Holy Spirit to make it happen. The Christian thinker Dietrich Bonhoeffer wrote a book on Christian community entitled *Life Together*.[4] In it he says that true Christian community does not occur naturally. Even with the same unified beliefs, people do not necessarily become harmonious. Instead, Bonhoeffer tells us that true Christian community only comes as a result of God's grace. He describes such community as being like a miracle that takes place as God brings together those who would not otherwise have come together as a group.[5] People's best intentions do not make community happen. It doesn't happen merely by having an expert come in to tell a group of Christians how to live and work together in peace. It is ultimately the work of Christ that enables true Christian community to take place.[6]

Paul directs the Corinthian church to Christ as the answer to their lack of unity. What is interesting is that Paul's own name was mixed up with the splits facing the church. Paul's response is to tell the church: "When one of you says, 'I follow Paul,' and another, 'I follow Apollos'—aren't you acting like worldly people?" (1 Corinthians 3:4 TEV). It must have been a temptation for Paul himself to feel that he had a large loyal following in the church. How easy it would be to resolve the conflict by implying that those loyal to him were right and the others wrong. Yet Paul says, "I planted the seeds, Apollos watered them, but God made them sprout and grow. What matters is not those who planted or watered, but God who made the plants grow" (1 Corinthians 3:6–7 CEV). He resists the temptation to build his own loyal following or increase his popularity. His mission is clear: to play whatever role God has for him in building up the Church to be a loving community of faith. Unlike the modern competition found between many churches and tele-evangelists, Paul is not in a rivalry with Apollos or other early church leaders. He acknowledges their work and calling.

Unity With Diversity

Affirming the different gifts people have within the Christian community is found again in 1 Corinthians 12. Here we read: "We can each do different things. Yet the same God works in all of us and helps us in everything we do. The Spirit has given each of us a special way of serving others." (1 Corinthians 12:6–7 CEV). Paul goes on to say, "Together you are the body of Christ. Each one of you is part of his body" (1 Corinthians 12:27 CEV). These words are immediately followed by chapter 13 which emphasizes love as the outcome of this body-life of the Church.

Bringing together unity and diversity is the second principle of Christian community. Love expresses itself in the Christian community when real diversity comes together with real unity.

The problem of unity and diversity has been identified as a philosophical question. Groups and cultures take on value systems tending to hold up either unity or diversity. Bringing together a balance is most critical as the world addresses the issue of diverse cultural groups living side by side. Many conflicts in the world result as people swing between asserting either unity or diversity. When people push for unity, diversity tends to get smothered. When differences are asserted, conflicts arise. In *The Dust of Death,* Os Guinness notes that "the Christian is not forced to choose between unity and diversity... A balance is struck, relatively in the world and absolutely in God himself, for God reveals himself as already three-in-one in his Trinitarian unity."[7] We should see the Trinity as the foundation for an expression of both unity and diversity in the Christian community.

In 1971, I graduated from college and became involved in full-time work at an inner-city church on the West Side of Manhattan in New York City. At that time, my prayer was for a model Christian community that would be a witness to the diverse cultures found in this neighborhood. Many divisions in the neighborhood revolved around social class and ethnic grouping. To make an effective witness, a living demonstration of diversity and unity through Christ was needed. God answered this prayer as a community of Christians came together living in and around two adjacent apartments in a tenement building. Although not a large group, it comprised Jewish believers, a Columbia University doctoral student from Greece, African-Americans, those with Caribbean roots, and

Anglo-Saxon Protestants. We called ourselves "Beth Logos Harambee." This is translated as: "house of" (Hebrew), "the Word" (New Testament Greek), and "community" (Swahili). Bonds of lasting friendships were formed here as barriers broke down. We learned how to appreciate each other's cultural experiences.

A number of people came to faith in Christ through the community. A member of a black radical group—the same group my classmate was working for when he lost his limbs in an explosion—committed her life to following Christ. Through the Beth Logos Harambee experience, Jh'an Moskowitz was nurtured as a young Christian, going on to become a regional leader for the Jews for Jesus movement. Living in this diverse community also had its struggles. Yet it was through our inevitable conflicts that we became sensitive to one another's cultures and learned about our own weaknesses in relating to others. Although this community was not based in a church building and did not consider itself to be a church, it expressed a unity and diversity lacking in many churches.

Real Christian community is possible when we appreciate our diversity. People are not all the same. We come from different backgrounds and have different experiences. Whereas for the world these differences are reasons for conflict and tension, among God's people this diversity is the basis for something beautiful. It was certainly good for God to create humanity as both male and female. Love operates best when there are differences. But many Christians avoid diversity as they try to bring about unity. They seek unity by suppressing diversity, having everyone conform to one culture, and assuming their way to be superior. This is not the kind of community for which God originally created humanity. Beth Logos Harambee reflected a high degree of unity within diversity but, unfortunately, after a few years the community dispersed.

Covenant Relationships

Christian community requires another ingredient—a rediscovery of covenant, the biblical ordering of relationships. This kind of bonding is needed especially where modernity and urbanization are making their impact. Today's relationships have become more and more transient, reflecting the surrounding throw-away culture. Relationships formed among Christians also reflect these disposable characteristics. One now finds spiritual transients moving from church to church and fellowship to fellowship. They may move when the "thrill" is gone or when the costs and accountability become too uncomfortable. The investment such people make in the community is limited. They know within themselves that they can leave whenever they want to. Such transience drains the Christian community.[8] Others who had committed themselves in these relationships are left hanging. They now become anxious about investing themselves in future relationships which in the end may also prove very transient.

Covenant relationships are needed in response to modern culture's casual way of connecting. We find a parallel here with the trend to short-term romantic relationships and marriages. People are drawn to such transient relationships because they can enjoy quick benefits while avoiding the work and responsibilities involved in a long-term commitment. For churches, this results in a lack of accountability and discipline. This absence of church discipline was also reflected in the Corinthian church (see 1 Corinthians 5). We tend to resist covenant because of an inward rebellion sometimes masking itself as a need for individual freedom.

A connotation of legal contract comes to mind as people begin to consider entering into covenant relationships. Yet, rather than an expression of distrust, the Bible sees covenant as a deep expression of love. Marriage, a biblical covenant relationship, is what a man and woman enter into when they really love each other. The marriage covenant was never meant for couples with little trust in each other. Likewise, Christian community should embrace covenant not out of distrust, but as the ultimate framework for the most complete expression of love. As a "new covenant" has been established in Christ, Christians are to reflect this in durable, binding relationships with other Christians. Not only does true Christian community bring together a balance of unity and diversity, it also represents a balance between form and freedom as love is expressed in the structured context of covenant.

The qualities of Christian community—unity with diversity, covenant, and grace—stand in contrast to the relationships found in the world. This new community serves as a model to the world of what God intends for the human community. [9] For Christians involved in social concern, this new community gives the basis for our vision of people living together in peace throughout the world. The community also provides support and encouragement to Christians engaged in social activism.[10] This witness of Christian community is needed especially for ministry in today's urban world.

8

STREET-SMART MISSIONS

There were so many reports of muggings and robberies in the city that people were afraid to go out late at night. Unemployed youths roamed the streets and joined together in menacing gangs. People put extra locks on their doors and called for more police protection. In the schools, teachers and administrators faced drug abuse, teen pregnancy, delinquency, and mental problems. In the community, cries went out for improved housing, medical care, and better city services.

Amid tall buildings and teeming streets, the noise level was deafening. Automobile horns, arguments among neighbors, and disco music playing loudly through the night made a good night's sleep an enormous challenge. With the congested traffic, hectic business pace, and stench of factory and car pollution added to the throngs of people everywhere, tranquillity was not to be found.

New York? Chicago? Detroit? No. This was Freetown, Sierra Leone. A city on the west coast of Africa. This was the foreign mission field to which I had been called as a United Methodist missionary. It certainly was not what I had expected. All I had ever heard about world missions before I landed in Sierra Leone concentrated on rural areas. I had been active in community organization, housing issues, youth work, prison ministry, and creative urban evangelism in New York City, so I had reservations about the call to go overseas. How effective could this "city slicker" be in some small farming village in a developing country? It didn't take too long for me to discover that, although away from New York, I was *still* engaged in urban missions.

The urbanization taking place in Freetown is similar to that happening in many places around the world. In Africa, Asia, and Latin America, cities are exploding. Over 650 million people live in cities with populations measuring five million or more. In Sierra Leone, more than one-third of the people live in urban areas. The city of Freetown grew from 125,000 people in 1964 to over one million in 1994. The shock of this urbanization has been difficult for many people to absorb. This growth in urban population has not been reflected in missions activities; in the United States, most presentations of foreign missions still highlight villages, farms, fields, and forests.

The Great Urban Commission

Christ commissioned his disciples to "go into all the world and preach the good news to all creation" (Mark 16:15 NIV), yet mission groups and churches leave the city out of this calling. Here again, conformity to a cultural bias is at work, affecting the deployment of mission resources. Growing cities continue to be where more and more people are migrating. Although the cities may shine with thousands of streetlights, they desperately need more of the light that only the gospel of Jesus Christ can provide.

People outside urban areas often have an attitude of fear and disdain towards cities. Racial prejudice and urban flight are reflected in many white churches in the United States. This has resulted in cities not being considered as desirable or exciting a challenge as rural areas when it comes to either home or foreign missions.[1]

This has not always been the case. Dwight Moody, the great American evangelist, devoted his life to ministering in the cities of the world. He once said that the Church must reach the city because it is the city which either infects the nation as a cesspool or nourishes the nation as a refreshing stream. Many Christians today act more like Jonah than Moody. They pick up and go in the opposite direction when God calls them to witness to the city. Ninevah was called a great and important city in the Book of Jonah—it was so large, it took three days to get across town (Jonah 3:3 NRSV). It seems they had rush-hour congestion even back then! Today, Christians are running away from their Ninevahs, fleeing to suburban getaways or flying off to the (rural) ends of the earth.

Mission means not only going to where the people are, but also demonstrating God's love to the people who are there.

Even after Jonah went to Ninevah, he showed a lack of compassion and concern, getting more involved in the life of a plant than in the welfare of the people of the city. God tells Jonah, "Ninevah has more than a hundred and twenty thousand people who cannot tell their right hand from their left, and many cattle as well. Should I not be concerned about that great city?" (Jonah 4:11 NIV). God is bringing His servants back to the urban world they, like Jonah so many years before, have been avoiding. One way this is happening is through the spreading influence of urban culture, moving far beyond commonly recognized city limits into suburban and even rural seclusions.

It was intriguing to see the reaction of many Western-world missionaries in Sierra Leone when they had to stay in Freetown for even a short period of time. Visibly uncomfortable, they sought to escape back to their rural missionary residences as soon as they could. I was hearing the same sentiments I had heard voiced by many non-city Christians towards New York City, especially regarding the blighted areas of the inner city.

Many Christians in lesser developed nations, together with ethnic minority Christians in the United States, are steps ahead in carrying out the type of mission required for the next century. In the urban communities of the United States, African-American, Hispanic, East Asian, and other ethnic churches have been left to carry out the work of urban mission with little help from those who have fled. Among the growing churches in Africa, Asia, and Latin America, one doesn't find anticity attitudes such as those found within so many churches in United States. The amazing thing is that so many of these urban churches are meeting the challenge while relying on limited financial resources.[2]

There is a need for urban Christians in Western nations to realize their own place in world missions. This can be difficult, with the pressing needs of their own neighborhood staring them in the face every day. Living in a city like New York City, with its cultural diversity and its desperate cry for wholistic ministry, it is difficult to see the world beyond. But cities much larger in population than the "Big Apple" exist—such as São Paulo, Brazil. Bursting with millions more than New York's eight million, São Paulo is expected to swell to twenty million within the next few years. Today, few would-be missionaries from the United States have to learn about farming and other rural skills in order to prepare for overseas missionary work. Most skills in demand can be cultivated in urban neighborhoods. Having only limited small town or farming experience can even be an impediment in today's growing urban world.

Churches and mission agencies should also be focusing resources on urban America—as an area to prepare missionaries, and because "the ends of the world" can be found in many American cities.[3] New York City, for example, is a microcosm of the entire world. One finds representatives of nearly every nationality living there. This diversity is reflected in the colleges; a recent survey showed that at New York's City College, almost one half of the student population was born outside of the United States, and represented more than seventy countries.

While I was in Sierra Leone, the newspaper featured the story of a Sierra Leonean student who went to New York City for a college education. This student soon developed financial and social problems, and ended up a derelict. Friendless, homeless, and without any family support, he committed suicide. Many incidents similar to this confirm the interconnection between world mission and urban mission in the United States. Because vast resources are needed to send people overseas, one wonders if resources could be used more effectively if given to support the work of such organizations as InterVarsity Christian Fellowship in New York City. The late Tom Skinner talked about the hypocrisy of many white Christians who claimed a commitment to mission. He said that while they would spend millions of dollars to send missionaries to reach black people across the sea, they would not spend one dime to cross the street of their own town to talk to a group of black people.

Potential world missionaries should be sure they are not bypassing their "Samarias" as they prepare to go to the ends of the earth (see Acts 1:8).[4] Our Samaria is those people who are snubbed by our own social group. They are the people we do not want to identify too closely with because of what other people might say.

The Effects of Urbanization

In Africa, another area where cities are rapidly expanding, the effect of modern urbanization on traditional culture may be more significant than the legacy of European colonialism. The traditional African is, in John Mbiti's words, "notoriously religious." This is because in traditional society religion is so encompassing, it cannot be separated from any area of life. In modern urban Africa, one finds a tremendous void in many people who thought the city would bring them a better life. But few ever consider returning to rural village living. This is because there is a captivating seduction about the city.

People can get so caught up in the city life that, even when faced with serious hardship, they remain. Young people in Africa continue to flood to the cities in spite of very high youth unemployment. People are attracted to the city for something more than material or social success. Although they may find themselves engulfed in poverty and other problems worse than in their places of origin, they refuse to contemplate leaving.

There are many parallels between urban America and the emerging cities of Africa, Asia, and Latin America; there are also many differences. Cities such as Freetown are not duplicates of urban United States. Traditional culture from areas near the city have been retained; most visitors are impressed by the vibrant sights and sounds of a rich, diverse African culture bursting forth from even the poorest areas. In the cities of Africa south of the Sahara, urbanization, modernity, and traditional culture have joined together to form a new social reality, comprising elements of all these influences.

John Mbiti described how traditional African religions and cultures were changing with the rise of modern African cities in his book, *African Religions and Philosophy*. He writes, "Most of the problems of the emerging society are concentrated on people living in the cities. There are [the problems] of housing, slums, earning and spending money, alcoholism, prostitution, corruption, and thousands of young people roaming about in search of employment. There are problems of unwanted children, orphans, criminals, delinquents and prisoners, all of whom need special social care to be brought up or integrated into their communities."[5] Originally, Mbiti saw this emerging urbanization as distinct from traditional African culture. Years later, attending a workshop with Dr. Mbiti, I learned that he had modified his views regarding the disintegration of traditional African culture within modern urban African. Noting examples such as the practice of traditional medicine in African cities, he saw traditional culture taking on a new form. Although traditional culture does persist, it is certainly not the same as what it is in the village. This is particularly evident among the young people who have flocked to the cities.

I helped develop the youth ministry program for the United Methodist Church in Sierra Leone, where many of the young people I encountered either came from rural areas or had parents who had migrated from up-country villages. In the decades of the 1970s and 1980s, young people made up a disproportionately large percentage of the rural to urban migration in Sierra Leone and elsewhere in Africa.

For the young people I encountered in the interior towns and rural areas of Sierra Leone, especially among those who had the privilege of education, Freetown was the place to be. There are many rural young people with experiences similar to someone we will call N'Guma Sesay. N'Guma grew up in a traditional rural family and attended a primary school in his village. Since he was a good student, his parents, both illiterate, agreed to let N'Guma go on to a secondary school in a town ninety miles away. His parents realized that education was a way to prosperity. They had seen the children of the eminent people in their village go off to school, then return as adults owning cars. They had built modern cement houses in the village for their relatives. As a result, N'Guma's family made the sacrifice of sending him to secondary school.

In school, N'Guma received more than a formal education. He also absorbed values quite different from those of his village background. Farming and traditional values were subtly discouraged. The desire to make money had replaced settling for subsistence farming. In no way would N'Guma consider marriage in the arranged manner, deciding now to wait until he was much older. Romance and sex were foremost in the interests of himself and his friends. He romanticized city life. N'Guma planned a way to go and live in Freetown. Even before his possible migration, urban values had already affected him.

Young people in the rural areas of Africa claim they are drawn to the city for economic opportunities. They also seek to avoid something. They want to get away from what they feel is the paralyzing influence of their rural roots. They not only want to escape the arranged marriages, but also the limitation of most of their lives being determined for them by family and village. They want freedom to be who they want to be. A similar drive brings young rural Americans to the city. Many believe that, in the small town, they can't be themselves. Everyone there already has a set picture of them. The city, on the other hand, offers one the freedom to be whoever one wants to be.

Urban society holds out to rural people a sense of freedom from the social constraints they seek to escape. This freedom is achieved through anonymity. In the city you can put on various identities almost as easily you put on clothing styles. You are not limited to the role branded on you from your childhood in a rural or small town society. Young people, especially, desire to pursue the lifestyle of their own choosing. On the other hand, the price to be paid for this urban freedom is isolation and loneliness. Community and social bonds are weakened by urbanization. For example, in urban Africa, people's ties to their extended family in the village are weakened. Life in the city means moving about as part of an anonymous crowd. No one has the time or energy to develop the kind of intense relationships generally found in nonurban society. Urban society is not supportive of close community bonds, including that of family and kinship. For many, life in the city is being part of the "lonely crowd."[6] As a nameless face in a crowd, one can easily feel like a nobody. An undersupply of love is part of what characterizes the cities of the world.

Spirituality and the City

Urban mission, whether in developed countries or in lesser developed countries, must involve understanding the needs of city people from a biblical perspective. We must explore what the Bible has to say about urban reality. Scripture speaks to the city in respect to spirituality, social relations, and lifestyle.

New York Theological Seminary has been dedicated to urban ministry for many years. The school has adopted a verse from the prophet Jeremiah as its theme: "Seek the welfare of the city where I have sent you into exile, and pray to the Lord on its behalf, for in its welfare you will find your welfare" (Jeremiah 29:7 NRSV). These are words to the Hebrew people taken into captivity in Babylon. They relate to the Christian presence in the city.

Babylon was known as a great and powerful city, a major center of culture, economic activity, and political life. It could certainly be described as a "world-class city" of its day, as New York, London, and Paris would be considered today. But it is not Zion. It is not Jerusalem, a city set up to be as God's throne (see Jeremiah 3:17). Babylon is a very different kind of city. In Genesis 11 we find that, at the beginning of history, the people of Babylon sought to dethrone God. The secularism of our modern cities also represents humanity's attempt to dethrone God. These cities are more like Babylon than Jerusalem.

In his book, *The Meaning of the City*, Jacques Ellul points out that throughout the Scriptures the city is presented as a place where humanity tries to exclude God.[7] Our modern cities are permeated by institutionalized secular humanism. Societies build cities under the premise of making life better. Yet, it is an unspoken truth that they also build them without seeking God's help. The city becomes a spiritual reality in which the Evil One's lie has a tremendous effect on peoples' lives. It is the lie that humanity can make it on its own without God. It is the lie that we can create our own secular and materialistic Garden of Eden; that we can resolve problems merely with technology, science, bureaucracy, and the other instruments of efficacy humanity has created. The cities of the world may hold great political, economic, and social power, but we find an absence of spirituality within.

The city is often represented as a place that is basically good or completely bad. It is either a place of dread from which any normal person should try to escape or it is an exciting place in which to live. "Inner city" often brings to mind unfavorable pictures of slums, crime, and broken families. When one lives in such an environment, the attitude we take towards the city is especially important. Some just accept urban life or even describe it in glowing terms. Others who have adopted very negative views of the city seek to avoid it altogether. Few adopt a "love-hate" relationship—which may be the healthiest of all responses. I find that those driven by such an apparent contradiction are generally the ones who make a positive difference not only in the city, but in the world at large.

The stance of urban Christians should be that of the Jewish people in Babylon: recognition that they are exiles. Just like anyone else, Christians too can become so caught up in the swarming activities and rushed hours of living that it becomes difficult to "sing the Lord's song in a foreign land."[8] In cities crammed with a flurry of activities, it is easy to forget God. Years ago some of my friends gave a name to the experience of returning to their city neighborhoods after being away in the country on spiritual retreats. They called it "urban shock." People tend to forget about spiritual values in their attraction to the city, and they tend to neglect their kinship ties. While rarely the stated intention of urbanites, it happens nonetheless.

Importing Some of Heaven into the City

God has a purpose for Christians in the city other than mere escape from or conformity to it. Christians are to live the lifestyle of the New Jerusalem within the Babylons of the world. The need for spirituality, community, and a wholesome lifestyle are addressed by the gospel of Christ. Jacques Ellul points out that, before the Fall, God had placed Adam and Eve in a garden. Yet, in Revelation we find a city, the New Jerusalem, as the final home for God's people. (Revelation   21:2 ff. NIV) In God's infinite grace, a creation of humanity devised from rebellion is transformed for His eternal plan and purposes.

In the Book of Revelation, the New Jerusalem is described as a city coming out of heaven from God. It is not created on earth or built by people. It is made in heaven. It is a city which only God can put together. The New Jerusalem will be a city filled with love and peace, saturated with the presence of God. Rather than a place of pain and suffering, it will be a place of comfort where God will wipe away all tears from our eyes. In order to build up our cities today in the way God desires, one would have to import building materials originating from heaven.

When Christians truly live out the lifestyle of the kingdom of God, others around have difficulty figuring out from where it originates, its source. It is like the various styles of clothing people buy in stores. There are tags identifying the country of origin. One may say "Made in France" or "Made in Italy" or "Made in the USA." People can become so familiar with the different styles that they are even able to identify the countries of origin without reading the labels. When the Christian lifestyle is demonstrated in the cities of the world, others are unable to trace it to any particular country of origin on earth. This is because the only tag it can be given is the one that says "Made in Heaven."

Many African-American militants back in the 1960s interpreted talk of heaven as an escape making oppressed people passive. Yet in many urban neighborhoods of the United States today, most people would welcome more of the love and peace of heaven amid the widespread crime, gang violence, and other destructive behavior of the big city. Like the Hebrew people in Babylon, Christians in the city are called to "seek the welfare of the city." Other translations say "pray for the peace of the city." The word "welfare" or "peace" can be translated to the Hebrew word "shalom." True peace begins with reconciliation to God and results in mental, social, and physical well-being. Christians are called to live a transformed lifestyle reflecting heaven. Today this call is for many more to go—or to stay—to minister wholistically in the growing cities of our world.

9

CHRISTIANS IN THE HUMAN SERVICES

A few years ago, I sought to recruit staff workers for a new homeless shelter for single men. I had just become the director of this program which was to combine rehabilitation with basic sheltering services. The program had originated as a local church's response to the growing problem of homelessness in their community. The church had set up a not-for-profit agency which in turn was awarded a government contract for this shelter. As one way of advertising the job positions, I made contact with a few local churches. Surely some people in these churches would welcome this opportunity to serve people who didn't have a home to call their own, I reasoned.

But this was not always the case, and especially not for one local church I phoned. They were known to be an evangelical church that took the Bible seriously. While talking with a church official, I was asked whether or not hiring was limited to only evangelical Christians. When I told them it was a government-funded program, the response was a refusal to help locate possible staff workers. As the program developed, many local religious groups contributed volunteers, clothing, and meals. The evangelical church did not contribute anything, and spurned a specific request for help. It seemed to me that they were boycotting the shelter, and I gathered that they felt those who supported the shelter program were doing something morally and spiritually wrong. Unfortunately, such a reaction is not all that unusual for a significant segment of Christians. It raises some issues regarding the involvement of Christians in human service organizations.

Why shouldn't Christians become employed in secular schools and social service agencies? Not once have I come across any written doctrines or official teachings indicating that it is somehow wrong for Christians to work for such human service agencies. Yet this is certainly implied by a number of people, particularly many white, theologically conservative Christians in the United States. Although this group rarely raises any issue about holding a job in a secular for-profit business, it raises strong objections when it comes to secular human service organizations. Why should Christians be discouraged from such employment when, it would seem, they have a stronger basis for entering this realm than do many other people?

The Great Reversal

Part of the answer goes back to the continuing artificial dichotomy between evangelism and social concern. For some, Christians are considered blessed when they become materially rich, not when they devote their careers to caring for and serving others. Another part of the answer can be traced to the influence of the Religious Right in the United States. They have aligned themselves with the secular conservative political push to drastically cut government help to people in need. Therefore, it would follow that individual Christians should be constrained from any involvement in government-funded social programs. When such conservative Christians hold these views while not establishing programs of their own to assist the downtrodden, they are, in effect, practicing a type of social Darwinism. Of course, they would certainly shun this label. Some within this group do have a genuine concern for people in poverty, but oppose social programs because they are "secular." Yet, even though secularism is very prevalent in other government operations and the business world, they do not apply the same logic to those areas.[1]

The roots of this withdrawal from involvement in the human service professions by the Christian Religious Right and some other evangelicals goes back to "the great reversal" in the earlier part of the twentieth century. Before that time, many Christians involved in revivalist movements took the lead in voicing concern for the disadvantaged of the society. The conservative Christians of this earlier time did not voice opposition to government assistance.[2] As was noted earlier, the split between evangelism and social concern is a phenomenon arising in the twentieth century and limited primarily to white fundamentalist Christians in the United States. There is another irony to this modern opposition. The historic roots of modern human service endeavors can be traced, in large part, to Christian promptings. In many ways, it was the Christian influence that brought about the establishment of hospitals, schools, and even various social service programs. The Salvation Army, the Young Men's Christian Association (YMCA), and numerous service organizations began as wholistic Christian ministries. In contrast to this, I have heard from various leaders of the Salvation Army that nowadays they have great difficulty recruiting professional staff motivated by their Christian faith.

Indeed, more Christians should be drawn to human service professions as a way of applying their faith. They should be attracted to work in professions aimed at serving people, especially those in need. At the time of the Last Supper, there is an argument among the disciples as to which one of them is the greatest. Jesus tells them, "The kings of the Gentiles lord it over them; and those who exercise authority over them call themselves Benefactors. But you are not to be like that. Instead, the greatest among you should be like the youngest, and the one who rules like the one who serves. For who is greater, the one who is at the table or the one who serves? Is it not the one who is at the table? But I am among you as one who serves." (Luke 22:25–27 NIV). People working in government jobs are sometimes labeled "public servants." The words of Jesus tell us of the general tendency of those in governmental authority to be self-serving, in spite of such labels. Jesus tells his followers *not to be like that*. Instead, they are to follow the example of Christ as one who truly serves. The implied call is for Christians to work in human service not as self-servers, but as sincere servants of others.

A Different Kind of Professional

The Reverend Tom Bangura, a bishop of the United Methodist Church in Sierra Leone, once told this story: A number of years earlier, a missionary doctor from the United States practiced in an up-country town. Although transportation to that place was difficult, large numbers of people traveled out from Freetown to see this doctor. "Why do you put yourself through such trouble? Aren't there doctors in Freetown?" he asked them. "Yes, there are many doctors in Freetown," they replied. "Is it because the doctors in Freetown do not have as much training?" he asked. They answered, "No, the Freetown doctors are very well trained." He pressed them further for an answer. "Then why do you travel such a distance?" The answer finally came that this doctor's touch was unlike the touch of any doctor they had known in Freetown.

When Christians live out their faith in human service, people experience a difference. Even in the public schools where there are specific legal limitations regarding the separation of church and state, a few Christian teachers stand out because of their special concern and dedication. They have that certain touch. For them, it is not "just a job." It is their way of living out agape love, the love from God experienced through Jesus Christ.

During the 1970s, it became clear to many of us committed to urban ministry in New York City that we needed some new strategies. In the midst of overwhelming problems facing poorer inner-city neighborhoods, there were so few examples of wholistic Christian service programs. While it was easy for some to berate humanistic secular programs, one rarely found any Christian alternatives. Tom Skinner expressed disappointment in regard to the reaction of many evangelical Christians when told about the poverty and the pain of living in Harlem. These Christians were unwilling to provide even meager resources to those ministering in communities such as Harlem. Many of us did find an alternative strategy for making an impact within secular programs aimed at addressing social problems. In the late 1970s, The Adolescent Pregnancy Care and Prevention Program (TAPCAPP) was born as a program that reflected this approach.

Transforming a Social Service Program

The development of TAPCAPP is a story of faith and vision. In 1978, Sheldon Nix, a staff worker with InterVarsity Christian Fellowship in New York City, brought together a number of Christian leaders involved in community-based youth work. He encouraged them to consider a new idea. Jimmy Carter was president at the time and the federal government had just announced a request for proposals of model programs addressing the growing problem of teenage pregnancy. Teen pregnancy was only then being identified as a national issue, as teenage girls were having out-of-wedlock pregnancies in higher and higher numbers. Researchers found that the problem cut across both class and racial lines. What they also discovered was that a great number of these pregnancies were intentional and not just the accidental result of sexually active teenagers. Some young women felt that having a baby would provide them with someone to love them. The baby would give them benefits that they were not receiving elsewhere in their lives.

Sheldon Nix brought together an interested group, but it lacked a specific plan for a program and the community in which to locate it. Barbara Brown, another New York IVCF staff worker, mentioned to Sheldon that I could possibly be of assistance. I met Sheldon at a small group meeting led by John Perkins. At this time, John Perkins was just beginning to contemplate the need for urban mission. Although he encouraged the group towards wholistic ministry, he explained that he himself didn't know how to reach people living in apartment buildings.

My family and I had just recently returned from our three-year missionary term in Sierra Leone on an extended furlough. I was completing a study program as part of the furlough, but was unsure about whether we would return to Sierra Leone or remain in the States and work in New York City. Weeks before, my wife and I had prayed that God would show us what to do by a certain date. This date turned out to be same date as John Perkins's meeting. Our prayer was answered, but not in the way we thought it would be. As I became involved with the group Sheldon Nix organized, the answer was for both short term work in New York and a later return to Sierra Leone. The mission board approved a proposal, allowing me to develop this teenage pregnancy project on the condition of an expected return to Sierra Leone. Others who became involved in this project had specific prayers answered in similar ways.

It seemed that just the right people came together at just the right time. David Grizzle, a Christian lawyer who had recently graduated from Harvard Law School, provided pro bono legal work for the project. A neighborhood in the southwest part of the Bronx was designated, and further confirmation was given as local pastors and Christian leaders in that area joined in the effort. A network was developed, laying the foundation to make TAPCAPP a reality. As details seemed to fall miraculously into place in spite of obstacles, there was a sense that God's hand was at work.

The TAPCAPP proposal involved a creative use of paraprofessional "big sisters." Most pregnant teens had to cope with a fragmented system of services, including health care, school, and various social service agencies. A community-based program was outlined by which teenagers would relate primarily to their own "big sister" instead of numerous impersonal professionals. These big sisters, in turn, would be supported and supervised by a professional staff.

This approach drew upon our critique of general human service programs. The trend toward professionalization in human service organizations resulted in removing the personal and compassionate side of caring for others. Such impersonal concern contrasts with a biblical perspective, where God and his servants dealt with people in a loving, individual manner. We also saw that some professionals were so wrapped up in professional titles that they were not able to see the potential of people without advanced degrees and licenses. By using big sisters, TAPCAPP embraced those with natural counseling skills who could serve as role models for the teenagers. At the same time, skilled professionals were assigned to insure quality work from the big sisters. TAPCAPP was to be characterized by a personalized style of caring which also discouraged professionals from looking down on nonprofessionals as a means of ego gratification.

Another answered prayer was the way in which the written proposal for TAPCAPP was assembled in record time. Only a very few people did the work of researching, writing, typing, and copying the proposal. Three of us worked through an entire night so that it would be completed by the following day. The proposal was taken to the airport at the break of dawn and was signed in at the Washington office only fifteen minutes before the legal deadline. It was later discovered that over two hundred well-established agencies throughout the United States had applied for this same funding. Yet, the screening committee was impressed by the TAPCAPP proposal, and it ranked at the top of the final selection. A field visit was made to insure the project was indeed feasible. Just days before the Washington group arrived, an ideal facility was found, located right in the middle of the target area. Walker Memorial Baptist Church had recently moved into a new church building that had an adjacent annex. The church had prayed that the annex would be put to good use. TAPCAPP was an answer to prayer for them. Although this was to be a large project, pieces continued to fall in place. The administrator of a nearby health center readily gave his support. A Christian medical doctor and other professionals volunteered to serve on the board of directors. When the Washington office team arrived, they were impressed. Although TAPCAPP was without any track record, it was granted 2.2 million dollars for its first five years of operation.

Small miracles continued to happen as staff positions were filled quickly. A large number of very talented young Christian professionals came forward. Months before the program was approved, my wife and I visited a woman we had not seen in years who was completing graduate studies in Massachusetts. During the visit she shared that she was completing a master's degree in public health. Not having heard anything about the TAPCAPP proposal, she said her area of specialty was teen pregnancy and she wanted to find a job back in New York City. Another person serving as an executive secretary for a wing of a hospital said she felt God calling her to leave her job in order to work at TAPCAPP. It meant taking a large pay cut in the process. Many other talented people came forward, seeking to put their faith to work in their employment. This made a difference in the program.

TAPCAPP was up and moving in an amazingly short period of time. Visiting government officials commented that they found the program's atmosphere to be very different from that of other programs they had known. We knew that the things we were doing—such as a daily prayer circle held fifteen minutes before staff signed in to work—had much to do with that difference. Many of the staff members were not committed as Christians, but they were affected in a very positive way by what was taking place. A sense of community and togetherness developed among the staff. While there were many problems and conflicts, prayer and application of faith conditioned the way in which those problems were addressed.

TAPCAPP was an example of the transformation of a government initiative into a powerful witness. Although TAPCAPP was not an evangelistic organization, it was a place where Christians brought their faith to bear on their professional work. The program also accomplished something constructive with respect to the issue of abortion. It provided an alternative by helping pregnant teenagers go to full term and delivery. Follow-up studies conducted years later showed that because of the services received from TAPCAPP, many of the adolescents did not go on to have more babies as unmarried teenagers. TAPCAPP taught parenting skills and helped teenagers to accomplish educational and employment goals. The program fulfilled its role as a model program, with the concept of big sisters becoming a widely recommended approach to addressing the problem of teen pregnancy.[3]

Much of the success of TAPCAPP was due to the fact that the program sought only staff demonstrating excellence in their professional work. Too often, shoddy work performance is excused by Christian organizations because the employee is said to be a committed Christian. When working in human services, Christians should be motivated to the highest professional standards. They should be continuing to study and master their craft. There should be full recognition of the professional excellence of any employee, not only of those claiming to be Christians. Sadly, both at TAPCAPP and in other situations, I have had to remove Christians who talked a lot about their beliefs, yet did not measure up in quality of work. A person called to human services should always be open to growth, learning from both Christians and non-Christians about professional qualities of excellence and integrity. We Christians need a humility within as we carry out our work. The original meaning of the word "professional," one who practices what he or she preaches, needs to be rediscovered.

While in Africa, I found many people reflecting on the Christian transformation of traditional culture. Through the TAPCAPP experience, it became clear that social service programs have their own "cultures" in need of transformation.[4] This transformation involves prayer, discernment, and putting faith to work. It also means the evaluation of programs beyond their labels. This was a lesson I learned years earlier while studying under Dr. Bill Iverson at New York Theological Seminary. As part of our studies, our class divided up and spent a night at different Christian mission shelters around the New York area. The students were not to let it be known that they were, in fact, not really homeless. The objective was to experience what it was like for people to come to those shelters for help. In the next class session, we compared our experiences.

What was striking was how much the shelters varied in their quality of service, although all were sponsored by Christian organizations. Some of us came away feeling a genuine sense of love exhibited by particular shelters. Others felt that the shelters they "visited" demeaned and devaluated the people who came for help. While all of these programs employed only Christian workers, the quality of service varied significantly. The experience of feeling what it was like to be on the receiving end made a lasting impression on me. It helped me years afterwards in the work of developing social service programs, particularly a shelter for homeless men.

Pessimists Acting Like Optimists

Many of those who get involved in social action programs do so out of the belief that they are changing the world for the better. They are optimistic that, with enough effort and with others joining in, social ills will eventually be eliminated. But this optimism is neither supported by Scripture nor by human history. "What has been will be again, what has been done will be done again; there is nothing new under the sun," we read in Ecclesiastes 1:9 (NIV). Our world doesn't really learn much from its history; the same problems continue to sprout up in new forms. While this realization may lend itself to a fatalistic dismissal of social programs as a waste of time, it should draw activists to find a firmer basis for their work instead. When activists are unable to respond to such pessimistic thinking, they themselves are vulnerable to despair. Many fundamentalist Christians also argue that working to alleviate social problems is a waste of time. They maintain that because we live in a passing age, Christians should only focus on a personal evangelism that highlights eternal salvation. For them, those engaged in social action are like people polishing brass on the sinking Titanic. Their position produces a result similar to the pessimist. In reaction, some Christians are inclined to be overly optimistic about changing the world in order to justify involvement.

Christians should be motivated toward social action out of obedience to Christ. It is essentially a matter of discipleship, not efficacy, that supports Christian social action. The analogy should not be that of someone polishing brass, but of someone doing acts of love and mercy while knowing all the time that the Titanic will sink. We can perform as if we are optimists even though we are pessimistic about the possibility of the world changing for the better. As Christians, our ultimate optimism is rooted in the kingdom of God. We live a here-and-now lifestyle of love and compassion based on an eternal perspective. A person can act constructively, though their actions seem like drops in a bucket continually springing leaks. We have a real foundation for showing love while others are preoccupied with an existential anxiety about life and death. Obedience, not success, is the bottom line for Christian involvement in social concern.

Opportunities Amid Limitations

In the United States, many Christians employed in government-sponsored programs face a genuine struggle. The doctrine of separation of church and state limits the incorporation of Christian evangelism in professional work. Yet it should be realized that this situation is not much different from that facing Christians working in the corporate world. In those businesses, employees are expected to represent the interests of the company. An employee working in sales would not be able to begin a conversation with a customer by asking about the customer's spiritual needs. One cannot use such a job as though he or she had been hired as an evangelist. However, Christians working within government-sponsored agencies and within the corporate world can focus on the opportunities that exist for demonstrating their faith rather than on these limitations.[5]

Christians are not immobilized from making a difference, even when specific government regulations are in effect. In any job, there are always openings for friendship evangelism with coworkers. There may also be openings for informal interpersonal communication with the people we serve. And there is always the opportunity to demonstrate a quality of professionalism which people will see as an "out-of-this-world" difference. Paul tells the Christians in Galatia to "live by the Spirit," and then he lists the fruits of the Spirit: "love, joy, peace, patience, kindness, goodness, faithfulness, gentleness and self-control. Against such things there is no law" (Galatians 5:22–23 NIV). There is "no law" restraining Christians from living out these fruits of the Spirit as we work within the public schools or in other government-sponsored programs.[6] The word will get out. As Christians reflect a consistent heavenly lifestyle, others will want to know how to live the same way.

Spirituality and Action

Regular prayer and Bible study are essential for Christians involved in social concern and human service professions. A heavenly lifestyle is not possible outside of a close relationship with our Father in heaven. Too many times Christians who want to get involved in social action are all too eager to run out and "do something." Unfortunately, many people have an image of a Christian activist as someone without time for prayer and spiritual reflection. The issues involved in social action are extremely complex. What may seem like an answer to one particular problem may turn out to make matters worse. Through prayer, we can discern between those actions which make a real difference and those which are ineffectual.[7] Many times, even before engaging in action, God may want us to get our thinking straight. This may involve praying for a purity in heart as we become engaged in social action or in a human service profession. As noted earlier, a person's motivation, although starting out right, can easily end up wrong.

Those involved in social action can be tempted by wrong motivations. It is easy to fall into the trap of helping the poor in order to score points with a particular social group. Some of us act out of self-righteousness, self-glorification, or other ego-boosting motives. Others may think that their good works alone will make them right with God. While it is difficult intellectually to admit to such reasons, ulterior motives always find a way of creeping in. A Christian's motivation needs continual examination in the light of God's will and purposes.

Christians involved in human service professions need the active support of their churches. Many pastors and church members speak about the need for their own church to "do something" about social ills. Yet, while considering actions as a local church body, they neglect those in the pew already involved in helping professions. These members of the congregation are, in fact, the church at work in the world. Local churches need to uplift them in prayer, affirmation, and emotional support.

Prayer is especially needed because of the forces encountered when trying to make a difference in the world. People find themselves confronting entrenched spiritual realities. One sees a little more clearly what Paul says in Ephesians: "For our struggle is not against flesh and blood, but against the rulers, against the authorities, against the powers of this dark world and against the spiritual forces of evil in the heavenly realms" (Ephesians 6:12 NIV). These are powers working to immobilize those fighting the evils of society. People like Dr. Martin Luther King Jr., Archbishop Oscar Romero, and others who have fought social ills have paid with their lives. A spiritual power of death reacts when signs of God's kingdom are evident.[8] Christians need to draw close to God in prayer so that they may become "more than conquerors" (see Romans 8:37). Burnout is often talked about by those employed in the human services. Human service workers need to draw strength from God and the Christian community to keep themselves going.

Christians involved either in the human services or in social action should pray for those they desire to help, and for finding the right approach to action. By trusting and drawing close to God, we receive inspiration for newer and more creative ways of serving people. Many people lock themselves into a particular way of dealing with social problems. This is true for many of those in the field of professional counseling. Through prayer and Bible study, Christians should be able to draw from many different approaches rather than locking themselves into one or another narrow school of thought. A Christian should be open-minded when seeking truth, realizing that much of what is put before them mixes both good and bad elements. I have found this to be true in the public debate over homelessness. Some people maintain that homelessness is simply the failure of our system to provide jobs and affordable housing. Others look at homeless people as failures who have neglected their personal responsibility. People tend to hold to certain narrow views that prevent them from seeing a more complete picture of the problem.

Tough Love

Christians should bring to this debate between social and personal responsibility a focus on God's kind of love—agape. The love Christians have for others should not be one that tolerates bad behavior as if it were okay. Homeless people do not need to be romanticized, or just given handouts. What is needed is "tough love." This love involves caring enough about a person to help him or her change bad conduct. Tough love desires for that person to be all that God wants that person to be. This response is one of reaching out with patience and long-suffering. It is a love that simultaneously comprises compassion and confrontation, challenging people to take responsibility for themselves.

A number of years ago, Bill Milliken felt called to urban ministry. He came to New York City and began working with gangs and other difficult teenagers on the Lower East Side of Manhattan. Through his work with these street teens, he learned that he had to be tough by drawing a line where it was needed. This did not mean that these youths would be changed merely by the presence of more police. Instead, a committed love and a real toughness went together. Bill Milliken later wrote a book titled *Tough Love,* in which he describes his experience with these troubled youth. Such tough love reflects God's love for us as individuals. How many times do we go out and blow it, not acting in the way God desires of us? While we know of God's forgiveness, we also recognize that God is molding our character. As a result of Bill Milliken's ministry, many young people had their lives turned around. Bobo Nixon, one of the gang leaders he worked with, committed his life to Christ and went on to become the director of the ministry Bill Milliken started. A number of years ago, I was privileged to get to know Bill Milliken and Bobo Nixon and gained many valuable insights from their work.

In addition to tough love, Christians can apply many other biblical principles to their work in human services. Among them are the importance of strengthening families, the recognition of cultural sensitivities, the need for effective management and stewardship of resources, and the provision of spiritual and emotional support for those working in the helping professions. Too many times Christians take their cues from fads or media attention. But as they apply biblical principles to their social concern and professions, Christians may have to take on unpopular positions. The stand of organizations such as Evangelicals for Social Action (ESA) in the United States is noteworthy in this respect. For example, ESA has adopted a consistent "pro-life" position on the issues of abortion, war, and the disadvantaged of society.

Conforming to Heaven

In *The Great Divorce*, C. S. Lewis gives a fictional account of a person who takes a one-day bus tour from hell to heaven. Before presenting the story, Lewis explains why the book doesn't include any scenes on earth. He answers the reader's question: "But what, you ask, of earth? Earth, I think, will not be found by anyone to be in the end a very distinct place. I think earth, if chosen instead of Heaven, will turn out to have been, all along, only a region of Hell; and earth, if put second to Heaven, to have been from the beginning a part of Heaven itself."[9]

When Christians bring some of heaven down to earth, the world experiences a taste of real revolution. On the other hand, choosing earth means tolerating and conforming to the world as if that is all there is. As Martin Luther King Jr. has written: "Living in the colony of time, we are ultimately responsible to the empire of eternity. As Christians we must never surrender our supreme loyalty to any time-bound custom or earth-bound idea, for at the heart of our universe is a higher reality—God and his kingdom of love—to which we must be conformed."[10]

Our motivation, strength, and style for social action comes from centering ourselves in Christ. Without him, we "can do nothing" (John 15:5). From this foundation of Jesus Christ and his heavenly kingdom, our social concern becomes unique, even radical. Os Guinness noted that "the day the [secular] radical falters is the day the Christian radical must demonstrate . . . staying power."[11] Such staying power is grounded in heaven rather than in anything on earth. And by living out the heavenly kingdom of God, we give the world "evidence of things not seen" (Hebrews 11:1 KJV). The *Contemporary English Version* uses the phrase "gives us proof of what we cannot see." We make visible what is otherwise invisible.

G. K. Chesterton once said that the greatest problem with Christianity is not that it has been tried and found wanting, but that it has hardly been tried at all.[12] When Christians take on Christ-centered living, it speaks to the world. People may not be convinced by preaching and intellectual apologetics, but it is difficult to argue with love in action. When we act as "living salt" in the world, we create in others that thirst which is quenched only by the living waters of Jesus Christ. By living a heavenly lifestyle, Christians offer a glimmer of that kingdom which will finally prevail in the end. In that promised New Jerusalem, there is again the tree of life, and its leaves "are for the healing of the nations. No longer will there be any curse" (Revelation 22:2–3 NIV). And no longer that inseparable mixture of good and evil so natural to our fallen world.

Notes

Introduction

1. InterVarsity Christian Fellowship (IVCF) is a student movement active on campus at hundreds of universities, colleges, and schools of nursing in the United States, and a member movement of the International Fellowship of Evangelical Students.

2. This convention is sponsored by IVCF and generally held every three years in Champaign/Urbana, Illinois.

Chapter 1 A Split-Level Gospel

1. Desmond M. Tutu, *Hope and Suffering* (Grand Rapids, Mich.: Eerdmans, 1984), 37.

2. David M. Reimers, *White Protestantism and the Negro* (New York: Oxford Univ. Press, 1965), 158. See also Columbus Salley and Ronald Behm, *What Color Is Your God?* (Downers Grove, Ill.: InterVarsity, 1981).

3. Glenn Usry and Craig S. Keener, *Black Man's Religion: Can Christianity Be Afrocentric?* (Downers Grove, Ill.: InterVarsity, 1996), 98–99.

4. See Salley and Behm, *What Color Is Your God?* 18–19. See also Carl F. Ellis Jr., *Free at Last? The Gospel in the African-American Experience* (Downers Grove, Ill.: InterVarsity, 1996), 44–45.

5. Salley and Behm, *What Color Is Your God?* 20–21.

6. Usry and Keener note, "It is now well documented that the first American slaveholders didn't want their slaves to hear about the Bible, because they were afraid the slaves would understand that Christianity made them their master's equals before God." *Black Man's Religion: Can Christianity Be Afrocentric?* 98.

7. See Eric L. McKikitrick, ed., *Slavery Defended: The Views of the Old South* (Englewood Cliffs, N.J.: Prentice Hall, 1963).

8. Reimers, *White Protestantism and the Negro*, 28.

9. Ibid., 50. Reimers points out that "in the years after the Civil War the churches were in the vanguard of those urging second-class status as a replacement of slavery for [African-Americans]."

10. Usry and Keener, *Black Man's Religion*, 100.

11. Salley and Behm, *What Color Is Your God?* 57, 81.

12. Ibid., 47-48.

13. Peter L. Berger, *The Precarious Vision* (Garden City, N.Y.: Doubleday, 1961), 110. Berger notes, "[People] want power, wealth, happiness, but they also want a theory which explains to them and to others that they are entitled to all these advantages. Religion frequently satisfied this need."

14. E. Q. Campbell and Thomas F. Pettigrew, *Christians in Racial Crisis: A Study of Little Rock's Ministry* (Washington, D.C.:Public Affairs Press, 1959).

15. Jim Wallis, *The Call to Conversion: Recovering the Gospel for These Times* (San Francisco: Harper & Row, 1982), 168.

16. Gordon W. Allport, *The Nature of Prejudice* (Garden City, N.Y.: Doubleday, 1958), 421. See also 413-426 and Allport's "The Religious Context of Prejudice," *Journal for Scientific Study of Religion*, 5 (1966): 447-457. Bernard Spilka observes that "Allport's designation of intrinsic and extrinsic forms of faith . . . still exerts a powerful influence 25 years after their introduction," *Journal of Psychology and Christianity* 5, no. 2 (summer 1986), 85.

17. Quoted in Allport, *Nature of Prejudice*, 416.

18. Jim Wallis, *Agenda for Biblical People* (New York: Harper and Row, 1976), 36. As Wallis notes, "Various authorities, institutions, political and economic powers, historic forces, ideological necessities, and social facts become idolatrous by demanding an absolute kind of allegiance and value and by coming between God and his people and by coming between people."

19. Usry and Keener, *Black Man's Religion*, 104-107.

20. David O. Moberg, *The Great Reversal: Evangelism Versus Social Concern* (Philadelphia: Lippincott, 1962).

21. Ronald J. Sider, *One-Sided Christianity?* (Grand Rapids, Mich.: Zondervan; San Francisco: HarperSanFrancisco, 1993), 21. Regarding Christian leaders in the Third World, Sider notes that "their ministry and theology often rise above the tragic one-sidedness of so many Western evangelical and mainline churches."

22. James H. Cone, *The God of the Oppressed* (New York: Seabury, 1975), 46 ff.

23. Miguez Bonino, for example, justifies a theological embrace of Marxism by maintaining that because "there is no *divine* politics or economics, . . . [we must] use the best *human* politics and economics at our disposal [Bonino's emphasis]." For Bonino, Marxist theory is the "best" socio-political analysis. He wrote these words in the 1970s, before the collapse of the Soviet Union. Miguez Bonino, *Doing Theology in a Revolutionary Situation* (Philadelphia: Fortress, 1975), 149.

24. Sider observes an additional weakness in liberation theology's tendency to limit salvation to purely socio-political reality. See *One-Sided Christianity?* 44.

25. Jacques Ellul remarks that, for most Christians engaged in social action, "our interests [are] confined to economic and social problems, *such as the world defines them, sees them and chooses to present them.* We put on the world's glasses in order to see only what the world sees. [The Christian] exhibits no clarity of vision which would permit him [or her] to see sooner, more deeply or further [italics his]." Jacques Ellul, *False Presence of the Kingdom* (New York: Seabury, 1972), 48–49.

26. Sider observes that "millions of people in former Communist countries are eagerly exploring Christianity, hoping that it will provide the foundation they desperately seek for rebuilding their societies." *One-Sided Christianity?* 189.

Chapter 2   A World of Good and Evil?

1. Regarding Genesis 2:16, Francis Schaeffer writes, "What was involved was the experiential knowledge of evil in contrast to God's telling them about evil." Francis Schaeffer, *Genesis in Space and Time: The Flow of Biblical History* (Downers Grove, Ill.: InterVarsity, 1972), 63.

2. Brian Griffiths writes, "[Each of these ideologies] . . . has what George Sorel . . . called the Myth. This is not an analyzable set of propositions describing the properties of the perfect society. Rather it is a partially defined fantasy, not susceptible to rational analysis but so powerful it stirs our emotions, forcing us to act." Brian Griffiths, "The Law and Order Issue," in *Is Revolution Change?* ed. Brian Griffiths (Downers Grove, Ill.: InterVarsity, 1972), 19–20.

3. Jacques Ellul goes on to note that this "myth was born with the explosion of marvels before the bedazzled eyes of nineteenth-century [people]." Jacques Ellul, *The New Demons* (New York: Seabury, 1975), 105–10.

4. Ron Sider points out that "some Christian organizations and churches major almost exclusively on evangelism. Others on social action. Each group uses the other's one-sidedness to justify its own continuing lack of balance, and the division devastates the church's witness and credibility." *One-Sided Christianity?* 15.

5. Sider, *One-Sided Christianity?*, 144.

6. A view such as that expressed by Stephen Carter would have been too complicated for many to deal with. As a law professor at Yale who knew them both, Mr. Carter affirmed that "both are serious people who have earned the intense loyalty of those who know them well." Stephen Carter, "Two Good People," *New York Times*, 13 October 1991.

7. Sidney Harris observes, "Adopting a middle-of-the-road position is usually just tepidity and timidity, but to grasp a paradox and to hold it in tension, requires courage and wisdom." Sidney J. Harris, *The Authentic Person: Dealing with Dilemma* (Niles, Ill.: Argus Communications, 1972), 40.

8. Walter J. Chantry, *Today's Gospel: Authentic or Synthetic?* (London: The Banner of Truth Trust, 1971), 19–22.

Chapter 3   Catching Humanity's Sickness

1. The first of Alcoholics Anonymous's (AA) twelve steps is: "We admitted we were powerless over alcohol—that our lives had become unmanageable." In recent years parallels have been made between the twelve steps of AA and biblical principles. For example, the group Friends in Recovery has adapted step one as: "We admit we were powerless over the effects of our separation from God—that our lives had become unmanageable." See *The Twelve Steps for Christians* (San Diego, Calif.: Recovery Publications, 1988), 3.

2. Regarding Adam and Eve's shifting of blame when confronted by God, Francis Schaeffer notes, "In a way, both Adam and Eve were right. Eve had given the fruit to Adam, and Satan had tempted Eve. But that does not shift the responsibility. Eve was responsible and Adam was responsible, and they stood in their responsibility before God." *Genesis in Space and Time,* 93.

3. Eldin Villafañe observes that "the texture of social existence reveals the presence of institutions and structures that regulate life, that seem to have an objective reality independent of the individual, and thus can become oppressive, sinful, or evil. We are all part of this texture of social existence, and our spiritual living is impacted by this complex web." Eldin Villafañe, *Seek the Peace of the City: Reflections on Urban Ministry* (Grand Rapids, Mich.: Eerdmans, 1995), 19.

4. Harold M. Baron writes, "Maintenance of the basic racial controls is now less dependent upon specific discriminatory decisions and acts. Such behavior has become so well institutionalized that the individual generally does not have to exercise a choice to operate in a racist manner. The rules and procedures of the large organizations have already prestructured the choice. The individual only has to conform to the operating norms of the organization, and the institution will do the discrimination for him." Quoted in Ellis., *Free at Last?* 150.

5. John Dawson, *Healing America's Wounds* (Ventura, Calif.: Regal, 1994), 30.

6. Reinhold Niebuhr, *Moral Man and Immoral Society* (New York: Charles Scribner's Sons, 1960). 8–9. Niebuhr observes, "The inevitable hypocrisy, which is associated with all of the collective activities of the human race, springs chiefly from this source: that individuals have a moral code which makes the actions of collective man an outrage to their conscience. They therefore invest romantic and moral interpretations of the real facts, preferring to obscure rather than reveal the true character of their collective behavior."

7. John White writes, "Western materialism assumes that matter is all that matters. Many people who would never consider themselves to be materialists in the strict sense of the term, nevertheless live as though material things were of supreme importance." And, "If our behavior (as distinct from our verbal profession) is examined, many of us who call ourselves Christians begin to look

more like materialists. We talk of heaven but we strive for things." John White, *The Golden Cow: Materialism in the Twentieth-Century Church* (Downers Grove, Ill.: InterVarsity, 1979), 38.

8. Sider notes that "biblical evangelism calls on people to repent of sin—all sin, not just some privatized list of personal sins. A biblically faithful evangelist will call on people to repent of involvement in unjust social structures." *One-Sided Christianity?* 176.

9. As Sider observes, "People [in North America] attend church but don't make Jesus and his dawning kingdom the center of their lives. Secular values effectively shape large areas of their thinking and living." *One-Sided Christianity?* 191.

10. Cone, *God of the Oppressed*, 159. See also 130, 157 ff.

11. Martin Luther King Jr., *Strength to Love* (New York: Harper & Row, 1963), 16.

Chapter 4   From Conformity to "Transformity"

1. *New York Times*, 14 August 1994, p. 1.

2. See Pius Wakatama's *Independence for the Third World Church: An African's Perspective on Missionary Work* (Downers Grove, Ill.: InterVarsity, 1978), 13–18.

3. H. Richard Niebuhr notes that for Christians seeking to transform culture, "the problem of culture is . . . the problem of its conversion, not of its replacement by a new creation; though the conversion is so radical that it amounts to a kind of rebirth." H. Richard Niebuhr, *Christ and Culture* (New York: Harper Torchbooks, 1956), 194.

4. According to Phil Reed, Christians should "apply mission theory and praxis to the 'hood.' " See Phil Reed, "Toward a Theology of Christian Community Development," in *Restoring At-Risk Communities: Doing It Together and Doing It Right*, ed. John Perkins (Grand Rapids, Mich.: Baker Books, 1995), 40.

5. Jacques Ellul, *The Technological Society* (New York: Vintage Books, 1964); see also Jacques Ellul, *Presence of the Kingdom* (New York: Seabury, 1967), 61 ff.

6. Eugene Peterson observes that the temptations "were the cunning attempts to get him off the track, every temptation disguised as a suggestion for improvement, offered with the best of intentions to help Jesus in the ministry on which he had so naively and innocently set out." Eugene H. Peterson, *A Long Obedience in the Same Direction: Discipleship in an Instant Society* (Downers Grove, Ill.: InterVarsity, 1980), 122–123.

7. In saying, "Man does not live by bread alone," Jesus quotes from Deuteronomy 8:3. Matthew 4:4 also records the second part of that scripture: ". . . but on every word that comes from the mouth of God" (NIV).

8. John White relates our materialism to a lack of faith as he observes that "*enslavement to the visible makes faith in the invisible suspect*." *Golden Cow*, 54 (his emphasis).

9. See Ellul, *New Demons*, 166 ff.

10. As White pointedly writes, "We worship a materialistic golden cow. At heart many of us have a greed for things. We have made the world's agenda of status seeking our own. Unquestioningly we have adopted the world's techniques of gaining influence and security. And it has worked. We are flushed with success." *Golden Cow,* 12.

11. See Niebuhr, *Christ and Culture*, 206 ff.

Chapter 5   Organic Faith

1. Sider, *One-Sided Christianity?* 194.

2. M. Scott Peck, *Further Along the Road Less Traveled* (New York: Simon & Schuster, 1993), 166-167.

3. Jacques Ellul, *The Subversion of Christianity* (Grand Rapids, Mich.: Eerdmans, 1986), 7.

4. See Niebuhr, *Christ and Culture.*

5. See Matthew 7:3-5.

6. Collin Brown notes, "For good or ill (and all too often it was the latter) philosophical ideas entered the blood-stream of medieval theology, and this in turn affected the life and thought of Christianity in later ages." Collin Brown, *Philosophy and the Christian Faith* (Downers Grove, Ill.: InterVarsity, 1968), 12. See also Francis Schaeffer, *The God Who Is There* (London: Hodder, 1968).

7. As Brown observes, "From Aquinas onwards it became accepted in large sections of the church that natural theology with its secular philosophical arguments provided the intellectual basis of Christian faith." *Philosophy and the Christian Faith*, 24.

8. See Ronald A. Ward's "James" in *The New Bible Commentary Revised,* eds. D. Guthrie, J. A. Motzer, A. M. Stibbu, D. J. Wiseman (Grand Rapids, Mich.: Eerdmans, 1970), 1222.

9. "The length of the argument in James [2:14-26] and its passionate tone shows that the writer is refuting an argument that at the moment was of burning importance, something impossible in Judaism." Curton Scott Easton, "James," in *The Interpreter's Bible* (New York: Abingdon, 1957), 12:43. Also see Ward, "James," 1222.

10. Easton, "James," 16.

11. Dietrich Bonhoeffer, *The Cost of Discipleship* (New York: Macmillan, 1963), 45-58.

12. Thorleif Boman, *Hebrew Thought Compared with Greek* (New York: Norton, 1960), 74, 171, 191-193, 202.

13. Sider also calls attention to this particular point: "In Western countries, at least, the greater danger today is cheap grace, not exorbitant grace. Our churches are full of people who somehow made a decision for Christ, or joined the church without any clear understanding or commitment to submit their

total life to Jesus as Lord. The result is a materialistic, sexually disobedient church that is so culturally conformed to the dominant values of Hollywood and Wall Street that one can hardly tell the difference between the church and the world." *One-Sided Christianity?* 113–114.

14. Cone, *God of the Oppressed*, 47–55.

15. J. Miguez Bonino, *Doing Theology in a Revolutionary Situation*, 88.

16. Sider, *One Sided Christianity?* 35.

16. Carl F. Ellis, *Free at Last?* 83 (his italics).

18. John S. Mbiti, *African Religions and Philosophy* (New York: Doubleday, 1970), 1–2.

19. Kofi Appiah-Kubi observes that "the concepts of Christology of traditional African Christians are practical, dynamic, living, and based on real life experience." Quoted in John S. Mbiti, "The Biblical Basis for Present Trends," in *African Theology en Route*, ed. Kofi Appiah-Kubi and Sergio Torres (Maryknoll, N.Y.: Orbis, 1979), 86. Manas Buthelezi contrasts Western Christianity and African Christianity in "The Theological Meaning of True Humanity," in *The Challenge of Black Theology in South Africa*, ed. Basil Moore (Atlanta: John Knox, 1974), 103. As an example, he claims that "the inconsistency between proclaiming 'unity in Christ' while at the same time failing to practice it is not as much of a problem to the Western mind as it is to the African."

20. Mbiti, "Biblical Basis for Present Trends," 87.

21. John Yoder points out that the New Testament word *pistis*, usually translated "faith" in English, might be better translated as "faithfulness." John Howard Yoder, *Politics of Jesus* (Grand Rapids, Mich.: Eerdmans, 1972), 226, n. 9.

22. "If one reduced the Atonement merely to Jesus' death for our sins, one abandons the New Testament understanding of the gospel of the kingdom and severs the connections between the cross and discipleship. The result is the scandal of professing Christians whose sexual practices, business dealings and political attitudes are no different from those of non-Christians." Sider, *One-Sided Christianity?* 95.

23. Ellul writes that, "Paul incessantly insists on the critical importance of practice. It is not for nothing that each of his epistles culminates in a lengthy admonition showing that practice is the visible expression of faith, of fidelity to Jesus." *Subversion of Christianity*, 5.

24. Bonhoeffer, *Cost of Discipleship*, 69.

25. See Ellul, *False Presence of the Kingdom*, 72–73.

Chapter 6   I Wasn't Listening to the Sermon (on the Mount)

1. Sider makes the point that "unless Matthew, Mark, and Luke are totally wrong, all who want to preach and live like Jesus must place the 'kingdom of God' at the center of their thought and action. This phrase (or Matthew's

equivalent, the 'kingdom of heaven') appears 122 times in the first three gospels —most of the time (92) on the lips of Jesus himself." *One-Sided Christianity?* 51.

2. Howard A. Snyder, *The Community of the King* (Downers Grove, Ill.: InterVarsity, 1977), 13.

3. See Villafañe, *Seek the Peace of the City*, 19–22.

4. Jim Wallis highlights this kingdom emphasis as he characterizes the call of the church as, "A new community of people who are being transformed by Christ. This means that, first of all and at the basis of everything we do, we must seek to become a kingdom-conscious body of people who, by their very existence and presence, call into question the values, assumptions and very structure of their world and free people to live in alternative ways." Jim Wallis, *Agenda for Biblical People*, (New York: Harper & Row, 1976), 107.

5. Clarence Jordan, *The Sermon on the Mount* (Valley Forge, Penn.: Judson, 1970), 22. Clarence Jordan is the founder of Koinonia Community, a group that gave birth to various ministries, including Habitat for Humanity. The community was a model of racial reconciliation and mutual caring in rural Georgia years before the beginnings of the civil rights movement.

6. As Sider notes, "Biblical evangelism calls on people to repent of sin—all sin, not just some privatized list of personal sins. A biblically faithful evangelist will call on people to repent of involvement in unjust social structures." *One-Sided Christianity?* 176.

7. Jordan, *Sermon on the Mount*, 19.

8. See Bonhoeffer, *Cost of Discipleship*, 121–122.

9. See Jordan, *Sermon on the Mount*, 25.

10. Psychologists have also identified this problem of self-deception. See A. A. Stappington's "Psychology for the Practice of the Presence of God: Putting Psychology at the Service of the Church," *Journal of Psychology and Christianity* 13, no. 1 (spring 1994), 8–9.

11. In Bonhoeffer's commentary on this beatitude, he writes that followers of Christ "have an irresistible love for the down-trodden, the sick, the wretched, the wronged, the outcast and all who are tortured with anxiety. They go out and seek all who are enmeshed in the toils of sin and guilt." *The Cost of Discipleship*, 124.

12. Jordan, *Sermon on the Mount*, 33.

13. Villafañe, *Seek the Peace of the City*, 3.

14. Ellul, *Presence of the Kingdom*, 28. See also 23–29.

15. Ellul observes that, "If a Church which is a mere association conformed to the propensities of the world, which is informed by the same ideas and prejudices, which follows the same sociological trends, is asked to be present to the world, that means nothing. It is merely a part of the world reuniting with the world. It will neither add nor change anything." *False Presence of the Kingdom*, 83.

Chapter 7   A Distinct Community

1. See Francis A. Schaeffer, *The Church at the End of the 20th Century* (Downers Grove, Ill.: InterVarsity, 1970), 138–139. He later writes in *True Spirituality*: "There should never be a moment when any generation can say, we see nothing [in the Church] of the exhibition of a substantially restored relationship between [people] in this present life. Every single generation should be able look to the Church of that generation and see an exhibition of a supernaturally restored relationship." Francis A. Schaeffer, *True Spirituality* (Wheaton, Ill.: Tyndale House, 1971), 165.

2. Barbara Benjamin, *The Impossible Community* (Downers Grove, Ill.: InterVarsity, 1978).

3. More on this caucus can be found in Benjamin, *Impossible Community*, 39 ff.

4. Dietrich Bonhoeffer, *Life Together* (New York: Harper & Row, 1954).

5. See Bonhoeffer, *Life Together*, 21 ff.

6. In *More Than Equals*, Spencer Perkins and Chris Rice write of their overcoming difficult obstacles in the process of racial reconciliation. They remark that "without God as architect, our plans for building reconciled relationships will eventually collapse under the weight of our old racial residue. . . . Only the kingdom of God provides the rock-solid foundation on which we can build reconciled relationships." Spencer Perkins and Chris Rice, *More Than Equals: Racial Healing for the Sake of the Gospel* (Downers Grove, Ill.: InterVarsity, 1993), 143, 150.

7. Os Guinness, *The Dust of Death* (Downers Grove, Ill.: InterVarsity), 226.

8. George Webber writes, "This laissez-faire optional nature of the Christian community is simply intolerable." He follows this with a call for covenantal relationships. George W. Webber, *Today's Church: A Community of Exiles and Pilgrims* (Nashville: Abingdon, 1979), 55.

9. R. Paul Stevens maintains that Christian fellowship is essential in the mission of the Church. He gives the witness of the early Church as an example and quotes from Tertullian: "It is our care for the helpless, our practice of lovingkindness, that brands us in the eyes of many of our opponents. 'Only look,' they say, 'look how they love one another. . . . Look how they are prepared to die for one another.'" R. Paul Stevens, *Liberating the Laity: Equipping all the Saints for Ministry* (Downers Grove, Ill.: InterVarsity, 1985), 103. Michael Green has said that "unless the fellowship in the Christian assembly is far superior to that which can be found anywhere else in society . . . the Christians can talk about the transforming love and power of Jesus until they are hoarse, but people are not going to listen." Quoted in Sider, *One-Sided Christianity?* 179.

10. See Wallis, *Call to Conversion*, 125 ff.

Chapter 8   Street-Smart Missions

1. Bill Pannell (now an associate professor of evangelism at Fuller Theological Seminary) observes, "A Vietnamese would have a greater chance to

meet an evangelical had he stayed home than he does by moving to the north side of Chicago." Quoted in Reed, "Toward a Theology," 40. See also Glen Kehrein, "The Local Church and Christian Community Development," in *Restoring At-Risk Communities*, 178. Glen Kehrein notes that "while recently some in the church are beginning to admit our inner cities are a mission field, only a very small portion of resources are committed to reaching the city inhabitants and even less to the inner city poor."

2. See Villafañe, *Seek the Peace of the City*, 29-39. See also page 37 where he calls the presence of the Hispanic churches and other churches which have remained in the inner city "a prophetic witness" to "the other churches and denominations who have left or refuse to enter" the inner city.

3. Phil Reed makes a call for Christians to "see the neighborhood comprised of many nations as a legitimate mission field and heed God's call to go to those places and make disciples." "Toward a Theology," 40.

4. See Ron Mitchell, "What's Next?," in *Believing and Obeying*, ed. John W. Alexander (Downers Grove, Ill.: InterVarsity, 1980), 19-24.

5. Mbiti, *African Religions and Philosophy*, 292-293.

6. This concept was developed by David Riesman in a book titled *Lonely Crowd* (New Haven: Yale Univ. Press, 1950). Although he did not write about cities in general, the term captures the isolation of urban life.

7. Jacques Ellul, *The Meaning of the City* (Grand Rapids, Mich.: Eerdmans, 1970), 52. Ellul sees the Bible presenting the city as a spiritual entity. He writes that "the life of a powerful city is but a constant succession of revolts against God." In the act of building cities, humanity "gave birth to something stronger than [itself]. She [i.e., the city] withdraws within herself, and spiritually becomes a closed and isolated world. . . . She excludes God because she is for herself her own sufficient spirituality."

8. See Ellul, *Meaning of the City*, 188 ff.

Chapter 9   Christians in the Human Services

1. As many conservative Christians withdraw from service programs, they tell other believers to stay away because these programs are now secular. Glen Kehrein points out that once Christians have abandoned urban service programs, "it is hypocritical then to decry the secularization of [these] ministries. . . ." "The Local Church and Christian Community Development," 168.

2. William Jennings Bryan is an example of someone who combined fundamentalist Christianity with concern for the disadvantaged during the early 1900's. Although now remembered as a prosecutor in the Scopes Monkey Trial, he had also been an influential spokesperson for liberal causes. Much of his opposition to the teaching of evolution came from the concern that it would lead to social Darwinism. He claimed that, even when practiced "unconsciously," social Darwinism was "antagonistic to the principles of

Christianity which make the strongest servants of humanity, not its oppressors." See Lawrence W. Levine, *Defender of the Faith* (Cambridge, Mass.: Harvard Univ. Press, 1987), 260–266.

3. As an example, see Barbara B. Blum, "Helping Teenage Mothers," *Public Welfare* (Washington, D.C.: American Public Welfare Association, 1984).

4. Al Dueck uses a similar parallel in relationship to Christian psychologists. He notes that "what is needed is a more discerning response rather than a wholesale rejection of culture or profession. Which aspects of culture are to be rejected? The professions need not be rejected en toto, but we must reject the implicit autonomy that cultures and professions tend to claim for themselves.... When absolutized, theories, practices and communities become the 'principalities and powers' of our own age." What he says could apply to Christians in other human service professions. Al Dueck, "On Living in Athens: Models of Relating Psychology, Church and Culture," *Journal of Psychology and Christianity* 8, no. 1 (spring 1989), 7–8.

5. R. Paul Stevens maintains that "unless we equip the laity to live all of life for God, Christianity will degenerate into mere religion." Later, he quotes Martin Luther: "There is simply no special religious vocation since the call of God comes to each at the common tasks." *Liberating the Laity*, 24, 85.

6. Vernon Grounds writes, "There is something highly significant—and most interesting—about Paul's catalog of qualities in Galatians 5:22–23. . . . These personality traits can be developed only through relationship and interaction with one another. They cannot be developed by hermits." Vernon Grounds, *Radical Commitment: Getting Serious about Christian Growth* (Portland, Oreg.: Multnomah, 1984), 73.

7. As Ellul observes, "Action really receives its character from prayer. . . . [Prayer] rescues action from activism, and it rescues the individual from bewilderment and despair. . . . It prevents his being engulfed in panic when his action fails, and from being drawn into activism, when he is incited to more and more activity in pursuit of success, to the point of losing himself." Jacques Ellul, *Prayer and Modern Man* (New York: Seabury, 1973), 172.

8. A small group of young Germans carried out a leaflet campaign opposing Hitler in Munich between 1942 and 1943. The authorities reacted by executing some members of the group. Others were sent to concentration camps. These courageous young people saw their struggle as a spiritual one. As they wrote in one leaflet: "True, we must conduct the struggle against the National Socialist terrorist state with rational means; but whoever today still doubts the reality, the existence of demonic powers, has failed by a wide margin to understand the metaphysical background of this war. Behind the concrete, the visible events, behind all objective, logical considerations, we find the irrational element: the struggle against the demon, against the servants of the Antichrist." Quoted in Inge Scholl, *The White Rose* (Hanover, N.H.: Wesleyan Univ. Press, 1983), 85–86.

9. C. S. Lewis, *The Great Divorce* (New York: Macmillan, 1946), 7.

10. King, *Strength to Love*, 11.

11. Guinness, *Dust of Death*, 366.

12. Peck, *Further Along the Road Less Traveled*, 200.

Suggested Reading

Bonhoeffer, Dietrich. *The Cost of Discipleship.* New York: Macmillan, 1963.

Ellul, Jacques. *Presence of the Kingdom.* New York: Seabury, 1967.

———. *False Presence of the Kingdom.* (New York: Seabury, 1972).

Ellis, Carl F., Jr. *Free at Last? The Gospel in the African American Experience.* Downers Grove, Ill.: InterVarsity, 1996.

Jordan, Clarence. *The Sermon on the Mount.* Valley Forge, Penn.: Judson, 1970.

Perkins, John, ed. *Restoring at-Risk Communities: Doing It Together and Doing It Right.* Grand Rapids, Mich.: Baker Books, 1995.

Perkins, Spencer, and Chris Rice. *More Than Equals: Racial Healing for the Sake of the Gospel.* Downers Grove, Ill.: InterVarsity, 1993.

Sider, Ronald J. *One-Sided Christianity? Uniting the Church to Heal a Lost and Broken World.* Grand Rapids, Mich.: Zondervan; San Francisco: HarperSanFrancisco, 1993.

Usry, Glenn and Craig S. Keener. *Black Man's Religion: Can Christianity Be Afrocentric?* Downers Grove, Ill.: InterVarsity, 1996.

Villafañe, Eldin. *Seek the Peace of the City: Reflections on Urban Ministry.* Grand Rapids, Mich.: Eerdmans, 1995.

Wallis, Jim. *The Call to Conversion: Recovering the Gospel for These Times.* San Francisco: Harper & Row, 1982.

Index

Index of Scripture References

Several translations were used in the making of this book. Where the versions are noted in the text, they are noted here.